GRADED
ENGLISH GRAMMAR
(INTERNATIONAL EDITION)
Book - 4

By

Ms. LATA SETH

(M. A. Delhi University)

DREAMLAND PUBLICATIONS

J-128, KIRTI NAGAR, NEW DELHI - 110 015 (INDIA)
Ph. : 011-2543 5657, 2510 6050 Fax. : 011-2543 8283
E-mail : dreamland@vsnl.com
www.dreamlandpublications.com

Published in 2013 by
DREAMLAND PUBLICATIONS
J-128, Kirti Nagar, New Delhi - 110 015 (India)
Tel : 011-2510 6050, Fax : 011-2543 8283
E-mail : dreamland@vsnl.com, www.dreamlandpublications.com

ISBN 978-17-3014-108-9

Printed by : RAVE INDIA

PREFACE

Here is a series on English Grammar for the pupils of schools. It has been prepared in a unique progressive manner and in a style that is quite off the beaten track.

The present book is meant for pupils of Grade IV who have just covered their lessons in Grade III. The lessons in this volume include Alphabetical Order, Semi-Consonants and Semi-Vowels, Nouns, Pronouns, Adjectives, Determiners, Verbs, Introductory It, Introductory There, Tenses, Vocabulary and Written Composition.

Illustrations have been used as the chief potent medium to teach the children basic facts of English Grammar. The author has taken pains to make the lessons quite interesting.

With intense pleasure, I place the series in the hands of teachers of the English language and the students hoping it will receive a befitting response. I am sure that it will serve its purpose in an admirable manner and create a place for itself over other books flooded in the book stores. Any suggestions for the quality enhancement of the book shall be welcomed and duly considered for inclusion in the subsequent editions to come.

— Ms. LATA SETH

CONTENTS

We have learnt how to write words in alphabetical order. In this chapter, we shall learn a new fact about this order. We know that **alphabetical order means the order in which the letters of the English alphabet occur.**

A. Look at the following pictures and their words :

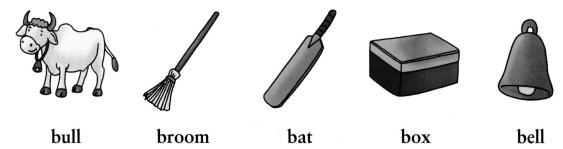

| bull | broom | bat | box | bell |

Each of these words begins with the same letter *b*. In order to bring these words in alphabetical order, we shall not consider this common letter *b* at all. Instead, we shall consider the second letters of all the five words. These letters are as under:

u   *r*   *a*   *o*   *e*

When arranged in A, B, C.... order, these letters will be—

a   **e**   **o**   **r**   **u**

So, the words written in alphabetical order will be—

bat   **bell**   **box**   **broom**   **bull**

B. IF THE FIRST TWO LETTERS ARE THE SAME

Look at the following pictures and their words :

| crow | crane | crest | cricket | crutch |

As the first two letters *(cr)* of all the words are the same, we shall consider the third letters of the words. These letters are *o, a, e, i, u*. When put in A, B, C... order, they will be **a, e, i, o, u.**

So, the words when written in the alphabetical order, will be—

crane   crest   cricket   crow   crutch

If the first two letters of the given words are the same, they should not be considered at all. The third letters of the words should be sorted out and put in *alphabetical order*. According to it, the given words will also come into A, B, C... order.

C. IF THE FIRST THREE LETTERS ARE THE SAME

Look at the following pictures and their words :

crown   crop   crocodile   cross   crotchet

The first three letters *(cro)* of the given words are the same, so, these letters will not be considered at all. Let us sort out the fourth letters of the words. They are :

w   p   c   s   t

If we write these letters in alphabetical order, we get—

c   p   s   t   w

So, the words, when written in alphabetical order, are—

crocodile   crop   cross   crotchet   crown

Similarly, if the first four letters of the given words are the same, they should not be considered. The fifth letters of the given words should be sorted out and put in alphabetical order. Accordingly, the words can be written in A, B, C.... order.

The practice in bringing words in alphabetical order proves very useful when one uses a dictionary for finding the meanings of words. We shall learn how to look up words in a dictionary in the subsequent book of the series.

A. Write the word for each picture and put the words in *A, B, C.... order* :

....	....	....
....	....	....
....	....	....
....	....	....

WORDS IN ALPHABETICAL ORDER :

....	....	....	....
....	....	....	....
....	....	....	....

B. Write each set of words in A, B, C.... order :

(a) name   nun   near   note   night

....

(b) meat   metre   mew   meet   mess

....

(c) string   strap   stroke   struck   stride

....

(d) throne   thrown   through   throng   throttle

....

C. Write five words all beginning with *ch*. Then put them in A, B, C... order :

....

....

D. Write five words all beginning with *sh*. Then put them in A, B, C.... order :

....

....

E. Write five words all beginning with *th*. Then put them in A, B, C.... order :

....

....

F. Mary has four friends as shown below. Write their names in *alphabetical order* :

Alfred   Misty   Tina   Chelsea

........1........   ....3........   ....4........   ....2........

WHAT IS A SYLLABLE ?

We pronounce words through *sounds* and write them using *letters*. Letters are either *vowels* or *consonants*. A word may have one or more vowels. Each vowel in a word may have *consonants* before as well as after it. This vowel and the *consonants* attached to it form a **unit of pronunciation**. This unit is called a **syllable**.

Observe the following examples :

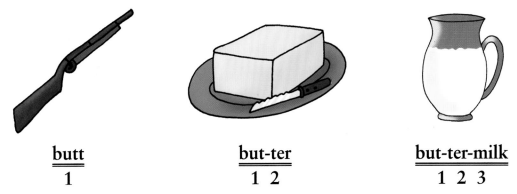

butt	but-ter	but-ter-milk
1	1 2	1 2 3

We clearly see that—

1. **butt** has only *one unit of pronunciation*. It is a full word.

2. **but-ter** has *two units of pronunciation*.

3. **but-ter-milk** has *three units of pronunciation*.

A *syllable* is a **unit of pronunciation forming a full word or part of a word.**

SYLLABICATION

We have learnt that a word may have *only one syllable* or *more than one* (two, three or four) *syllables*. In terms of syllables, a word is named after the number of syllables it has. Here are a few examples :

(a)	but	pen	hind	light	sin	silk
	1	1	1	1	1	1

Each of these words has **one syllable** only.

Such words are called **monosyllabic words**. **Mono** means *one*.

(b)	but-ter	pen-cil	be-hind	de-light	sin-ful	silk-worm
	1　　2	1　　2	1　　2	1　　2	1　　2	1　　2

Each of these words has **two syllables**.

Such words are called **bisyllabic words**. **Bi** means *two*.

(c)	but-ter-milk	de-light-ful	sin-ful-ness
	1　2　3	1　2　3	1　2　3

Each of these words has **three syllables**.

Such words are called **trisyllabic words**. **Tri** means *three*.

(d)	Co-ward-li-ness	un-sel-fish-ness
	1　2　3　4	1　2　3　4

Either of these two words has **four** *(more than three)* **syllables**.

Such words are called **polysyllabic words**. **Poly** means *many*.

The process of breaking up words into syllables is called *syllabication*.

TEST YOURSELF

A. **What is a *syllable* ? Give four examples :**

....

....

Examples : ....　.................　.................　.................

B. **What is meant by *syllabication* ? Give three examples :**

....

....

Examples : ....　......................　......................

C. **Syllabicate each of the following words. Also name it :**

　1.　seen　　　:　...............................　...............................

　2.　helpful　　:　...............................　...............................

4. milkman : ....

5. unselfishness : ....

6. student : ....

7. instrument : ....

8. confidence : ....

9. simplification : ....

10. sleeplessness : ....

11. unsystematical : ....

12. polysyllabic : ....

D. Here are a few pictures. Write the word for each of them. Also name it in terms of syllables :

....

....

....

....

VOWELS AND CONSONANTS

We have already read about vowels and consonants. We know that—

1. The English alphabet has 26 letters in all.
2. Five of these letters—**a, e, i, o, u**—are **voiced**. They have their own sounds and so they can be spoken freely. They are called **vowels**.
3. The remaining 21 letters of the alphabet are **unvoiced**. They do not have their own sounds and they cannot be spoken freely. So, they are called **consonants**.
4. Consonants can be spoken only when they combine with vowels. In other words, they become *sonant* (voiced) in the *company* of vowels. So, they are called as **consonants**.

SEMI-CONSONANTS

VOWEL SOUND OF U

Out of these five vowels, **u** has two types of sounds. As a vowel, it has its sound as in the following words :

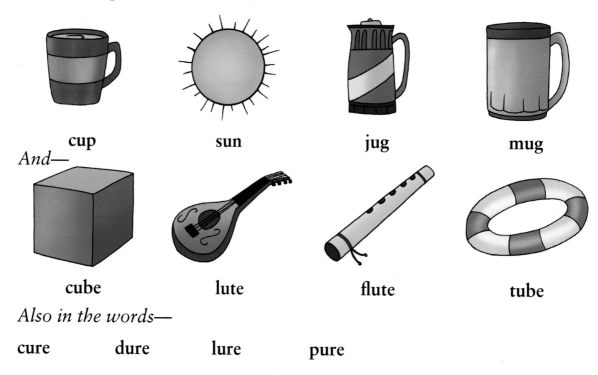

| cup | sun | jug | mug |

And—

| cube | lute | flute | tube |

Also in the words—

cure   dure   lure   pure

12

CONSONANT SOUND OF U

But **u** sounds as a **consonant** similar to **y**. It has its consonant sound as in the following words:

uniform

unit

urinal

utensils

Also in the words—

union **unison** **U-boat** **unity** **university**

We know that *u* is basically a vowel. But it sounds as a consonant as well. So, it is called a **semi-consonant**.

SEMI-VOWELS

We know that there are 21 consonants. Two of them are **w** and **y**. Either of these consonants has a vowel sound also. Let us study them one by one.

CONSONANT SOUND OF Y

As a consonant, **y** has its sound as in the following words :

yak

you

yarn

year

VOWEL SOUND OF Y

But **y** also sounds as a vowel just like long **i**. Observe the following words :

fly

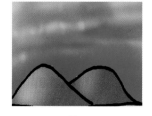
sky

cry

fry

CONSONANT SOUND OF W

We know that **w** has its consonant sound as in the following words :

| wall | well | wolf | watch |

VOWEL SOUND OF W

But **w** sounds as a vowel also just like long **u**. It has its vowel sound as in the following words :

| dew | ewe | mew | stew |

Also in the words—

| blew | crew | few | grew | jew | new |
| cow | how | now | howl | brown | crown |

We know that **y** and **w** are basically **consonants**. But they sound as **vowels** as well. So, they are called **semi-vowels**.

TEST YOURSELF

A.   Answer the following :

1.   How many sounds of *u* are there ?   ....
2.   What is the consonant sound of *u* like ?   ....
3.   How many sounds of *y* are there ?   ....
4.   What is the vowel-sound of *y* like ?   ....

5. How many sounds of *w* are there ? ....

6. What is the vowel-sound of *w* like ? ....

B. **Speak each word. Write the sound of its *u* under it :**

urn	unit	under	utility
....	....	....	....
umpire	union	udder	use
....	....	....	....

C. **Speak each word. Write the sound of its *y* under it :**

sly	year	sky	yellow
....	....	....	....
try	spy	yell	my
....	....	....	....

2008

D. **Speak each word. Write the sound of its *w* under it :**

why	blew	stew	vowel
....	....	....	....
work	crew	warm	well
....	....	....	....

E. *(a)* Write ten words with vowel sounds of u :

....
....

(b) Write five words with *u* having its consonant sound :

....

(c) Write five words with *y* having its consonant sound :

....

(d) Write five words with *y* having its vowel sound :

....

(e) Write ten words with *w* having its consonant sound :

....

(f)   write five words with w having its vowel sound:

....

F.   Look at each picture. Write the word for it. Also write the sound of *u* in it :

....
....

G.   Look at each picture. Write the word for it. Also write the sound of *y* in it :

....
....

H.   Look at each picture. Write the word for it. Also write the sound of *w* in it :

....
....

We learnt about *naming words* (nouns) in the previous book of this series. Nouns name *persons, places, animals, things*. Besides they name *feelings, actions, qualities, arts* and *states*.

All the things named by nouns fall into two groups as under :

1. Things **that have material bodies** *and* **can be touched**. Such things are **concrete**.

| chair | cow | window | king |

Clearly, concrete things include *persons, places, animals, things* etc.

2. Things that **have no material bodies** and **cannot be touched**. We can only *think of* such things. So, they are **abstract**.

| smell | race | sadness | strength |

So, nouns have two chief kinds.

1. Concrete   2.   Abstract

A *concrete noun* is the name given to a concrete thing.

An *abstract noun* is the name given to an abstract thing.

NOUNS

Concrete   Abstract

A. Answer the following :

1. What are things with material bodies called ? ....
2. What are things with no material bodies called ? ....
3. Which things do concrete nouns name ? ....
4. Which things do abstract nouns name ? ....

B. Define—

(a) a *noun* : ....

....

(b) a *concrete noun* : ....

....

(c) an *abstract noun* : ....

....

C. Given below are nouns naming various things. Which of them are *concrete* ? Circle them :

ornaments	success	children	vegetables	health
freshness	science	boy	height	chair
bravery	wealth	honey	plants	table

D. Put a *concrete noun* in each blank :

1. My .... is a leading doctor of the town.
2. The Taj Mahal stands on the bank of the ....
3. The .... sold all his articles in an hour.
4. Big cats include .... and tigers.
5. Trees bring forth new .... during spring.
6. A bad .... quarrels with his tools.
7. The sun is a .... like other stars in the sky.

E. Each sentence has a noun. Sort it out and write it in the blank. Also name its kind :

	Sentences	Nouns	Kinds
1.	Your frock is very dirty.	....	....
2.	The lion is prowling about.	....	....
3.	Real beauty is very rare.	....	....
4.	Don't hide your faults.	....	....
5.	I like eating green vegetables.	....	....
6.	Let's go to the zoo today.	....	....
7.	Honesty never goes unrewarded.	....	....
8.	Jokers make all of us laugh.	....	....
9.	Plants are very useful to us.	....	....

F. Each sentence has two nouns—one *concrete* and the other *abstract*. Sort them out and write them in their blanks :

1. Hitler was a ruthless dictator.

   concrete : ....   *abstract* : ....

2. Politeness can win even a cruel man.

   concrete : ....   *abstract* : ....

3. I lost my parents in my childhood.

   concrete : ....   *abstract* : ....

4. Mary has a very fair complexion.

   concrete : ....   *abstract* : ....

5. Cleanliness is loved by all people.

   concrete : ....   *abstract* : ....

6. Japan produces largest number of cars.

   concrete : ....   *abstract* : ....

FOUR TYPES OF CONCRETE NOUNS

We know that concrete nouns name things that have material bodies and can be touched. Such things fall into four groups :

1. Things with a *common name*.
2. Things with *particular names*.
3. Things *that are materials*.
4. Things that *name collections* or *groups*.

So, concrete nouns are of four kinds :

1. Common Noun 2. Proper Noun   3. Material Noun 4. Collective Noun

CONCRETE NOUNS

| COMMON NOUN | PROPER NOUN | MATERIAL NOUN | COLLECTIVE NOUN |

In this chapter, we shall study **common noun** and **proper noun**.

COMMON NOUN

Observe these sentences :

1. A **pen** is to write with.
2. **Dogs** are very faithful.
3. We worship in **churches**.
4. **Birds** can walk as well as fly.

In these sentences—

1. The noun—**pen**—is a *common name* for all the pens in the world.
2. The noun—**dogs**—stands as a *common name* for all the dogs.
3. The noun—**churches**—is a *common name* for all the churches.
4. The noun—**birds**—is a *common name* for all the birds in the world.

Each of these nouns is a *common* name for all the things of its class. Its usage denotes for a group of things. That is why it is called a **common noun**.

A *common noun* is the name common to all the things in a class or group.

PROPER NOUN

Observe these sentences :

1. **Rover** is our pet dog.
2. **Eiffel Tower** is in Paris.
3. **USA** is a developed country.
4. **Bob** is a tall hefty young man.

In these sentences :

1. **Rover**—is a dog with a *particular name*.
2. **Eiffel Tower**—is a *particular name* in Paris.
3. **USA**—is a *particular name* given to a country.
4. **Bob**—is a *particular name* given to a man.

All these words are **particular** or **proper** names given to various common nouns. So, they are called **proper nouns**.

> **A *proper noun* is a particular name given to a common noun.**

Remember that—

1.Each proper noun is written with its first letter capital.

2.Proper nouns name the following things :

(a)	Books	: Merchant of Venice, Passage to England
(b)	Mountains	: The Rockys, the Andes
(c)	Oceans	: The Atlantic Ocean, the Pacific Ocean
(d)	Seas	: The Caspian Sea, the Black Sea
(e)	Trains	: The Orient Express, the Pacific Express
(f)	Rivers	: The Nile, the Thames
(g)	Newspapers	: The New York Times, the Mail
(h)	Towns	: London, Tokyo, Moscow

TEST YOURSELF

A. Write five *proper nouns* and use them in your sentences :

1. .... : ....

2.   ....: ....

3.   ....: ....

4.   ....: ....

5.   ....: ....

B. Each picture shows a *common noun*. Write the word for it and make a sentence :

....

1.   ....

2.   ....

3.   ....

4.   ....

5.   ....

C. Column A has a list of *common nouns*. Column B has a list of *proper nouns*. Pair them in a suitable way :

A	B
Girl	Mount Everest
Country	Thames
Newspaper	Reebok
Book	Germany
Shoes	Jennifer
River	The Sun
Peak	The Bible

D. Pick out *proper nouns* and write them in the blanks :

1. The river Nile is in Egypt.   ....

2. Hitler was a cruel dictator.   ....

3. The Americans are brave people. ....

4. Egypt is an ancient city. ....

5. We stayed in the Buckingham Palace. ....

6. Nelson Mandela is a great leader. ....

7. We went to the Jurassic Park. ....

8. Have you ever been to the Taj Mahal ? ....

9. Tommy was a faithful dog. ....

10. Plaza Hotel is a big hotel. ....

E. Each sentence has a *common noun* and also a *proper noun*. Sort them out and write them in their columns :

Sentences	P. Nouns	C. Nouns
1. James was a great magician.	....	....
2. Australia is the smallest continent.	....	....
3. Julia is a fine actress.	....	....
4. Napolean was a great ruler.	....	....
5. The Bible is a holy book.	....	....
6. Germany is the best land of all.	....	....
7. Aristotle was a great philosopher.	....	....
8. France is famous for its perfumes.	....	....
9. Malaysia is a beautiful country.	....	....
10. England is a small country.	....	....

F. Define —

(a) a *proper noun* :

....

....

(b) a *common noun* :

....

....

In this lesson, we shall study the remaining two kinds of concrete nouns. They are—

    1.   Material Noun   2.   Collective Noun

MATERIAL NOUN

Observe these sentences :

1. **Wood** is a very useful material.
2. Rings are made of **gold**.
3. Bricks are made of **clay**.
4. **Silver** is a costly metal.
5. Bottles are made of **glass**.

In these sentences—

1. The word—**wood**—is a material from which furniture is made of.
2. The word—**gold**—is a material from which ornaments are made of.
3. The word—**clay**—is a material from which pots are made of.
4. The word—**silver**—is a material from which ornaments are made of.
5. The word—**glass**—is a material from which bottles are made of.

Each of these words name **materials** used to make different things. Such names (nouns) are **material nouns**.

A *material noun* is the name of a substance (material) of which things are made.

COLLECTIVE NOUN

Observe these sentences :

1. There are 25 *students* in our **class**.
2. A **herd** of *cattle* is grazing there.
3. Where is the **bunch** of *keys* ?
4. Here comes a **bevy** of girls.

In these sentences—

1. **class**—is a name given to a group of *students*.
2. **herd**—is a name given to a collection of *cattle*.
3. **bunch**—is a name given to a collection of *keys*.
4. **bevy**—is a name given to a group of *girls*.

Each of these words names a *collection* or *group* of nouns. Such names (nouns) are called **collective nouns.**

A *collective noun* is the name given to a collection of animals, persons or things taken as a whole.

Note. 1 Remember that material and collective nouns are, in fact, common nouns.
2. A common noun naming a *material* is called a **material noun.**
3. A common noun naming a *group/collection* as a whole is called a **collective noun.**
4. Most collective nouns are treated as *singular nouns.*

TEST YOURSELF

A. **Pick out the *material noun* in each sentence and write it in the blank :**

Sentences	Material Nouns
1. Aluminium is a very light metal.	....
2. Tyres of vehicles are made of rubber.	....
3. Bread is made from wheat flour.	....
4. Crockery is made of china clay.	....
5. Many articles are made of plastics.	....
6. This goblet is made of glass.	....
7. Garments are made of cloth.	....
8. Cloth is made of silk or cotton.	....
9. Shoes are made of leather.	....
10. Boxes are made of wood or tin.	....

B. **Pick out the *collective noun* in each sentence and write it in the blank :**

Sentences	Collective Nouns
1. The audience gave him a loud clap.	....
2. Are you a member of this club ?	....
3. A swarm of bees attacked the hunter.	....

4. A group of labourers are at work. ....

5. The farmer sent for a faggot of sticks. ....

6. Elephants take shelter in groves of trees. ....

7. The shepherd is tending his flock of sheep. ....

8. A covey of partridges is in the paddy field. ....

9. He performed his feats before a crowd. ....

10. Our cricket team has won the match. ....

C. Each sentence has a *collective noun* and a *material noun*. Sort them out and write in their blanks :

Sentences	*Coll. Noun*	*Mat. Noun*
1. This tea-set is made of china clay.	....	
2. That pack of cards is made of plastic.	....	
3. This bundle of candles is made of wax.	....	
4. This crockery-set is made of ivory.	....	
5. This set of ornaments is made of silver.	....	
6. This lemon-set is made of glass.	....	

D. Column A has a list of *common nouns* while column B has a list of *collective nouns*. Pair them suitably.

A	B	
Soldiers	cluster	an army of soldiers
Lions	pack	....
Stars	shoal	....
Girls	clump	....
Fish	bevy	....
Trees	army	....
Hounds	pride	....

26

E. Write any five *material nouns* and use them in your own sentences :

Material Nouns   Sentences

1. .... : ....
2. .... : ....
3. .... : ....
4. .... : ....
5. .... : ....

F. Write any five *collective nouns* and use them in your own sentences :

Collective Nouns   Sentences

1. .... : ....
2. .... : ....
3. .... : ....
4. .... : ....
5. .... : ....

G. Fill up each blank with a *material noun* :

1. .... is the most commonly used material these days.
2. Modern furniture is made of .... or ....
3. Shoes are made of .... or ....
4. Ornaments are made of ...., ... or.........................
5. ...., ..., ... and ....
   are used to make buildings.

H. Fill up each blank with a *collective noun* :

1. The mother-hare bore a ....of three leverets.
2. There hangs a ....of ripe sweet bananas.
3. An ....of listeners assembled to hear the leader.

4. There are several .... of stars in the sky.

5. A .... of hounds chased the stag.

I. Define —

(a) a *material noun* : ....

....

(b) a *collective noun* : ....

....

J. Each sentence has four nouns. Underline them and write their kinds in the blanks :

1. Peter made his set of pots out of clay.

   1. .... 2. .... 3. .... 4. ....

2. Mac bought a packet of biscuits made of flour.

   1. .... 2. .... 3. .... 4. ....

3. Simon ordered a bagful of cakes made of flour.

   1. .... 2. .... 3. .... 4. ....

4. Veronica wore a pretty skirt made of silk.

   1. .... 2. .... 3. .... 4. ....

K. Use these *nouns* in sentences of your own :

1. marble : ....

2. packet : ....

3. iron : ....

4. flock : ....

5. plastic : ....

6. covey : ....

7. team : ....

8. red-stone : ....

We read about pronouns in the previous book of this series. We know that there are eight chief pronouns—*I, we, you, you, he, she, it* and *they*. All these eight pronouns are used mostly for **persons**. So, they are called **personal pronouns**. Let us read about them in detail.

PERSONAL PRONOUNS

The eight chief personal pronouns are as under :

| I | We | You (*Singular*) | You (Plural) |

| He | She | It | They |

We know that **I, we** are pronouns of the *first person*.

You (*singular*) and **you** (*plural*) are pronouns of the *second person*.

He, she, it, they are pronouns of the *third person*.

TABLE OF PERSONAL PRONOUNS

Persons	Number	Used as Subjects	Used as Objects	Used as Possessives
First Person	*Singular*	I	me	mine
	Plural	we	us	ours
Second Person	*Singular*	you	you	yours
	Plural	you	you	yours
Third Person	*Singular*	he, she, it	him, her, it	his, hers, its
	Plural	they	them	theirs

Personal pronouns are used in place of nouns to avoid their repetition.

Observe the following sentences :

1. My father is a wise man. **He** told **me** to be polite.
2. **I** must act upon his advice.
3. **You** can sit on this chair. **It** is **mine**.
4. Some children are careless. **They** often fail.
5. **I, you** and **he** are all to blame.
6. This book is **hers**.

The words in bold type—**He, me, I, You, It, mine, They, I, you, he, hers**—have been used for *persons* and *things*. So, all of them are **Personal pronouns**.

A *personal pronoun* is a word used in place of a noun that names a *person* or a *thing*.

PRONOUNS ENDING IN 'SELF'

There are words (formed from personal pronouns) that end in **self**. The table given below shows these words :

Person	Plural	Plural
First	myself	ourselves
Second	yourself	yourselves
Third	himself, herslf, itself.	themselves

These *self-pronouns* are used in two ways :

1. To *emphasize* the action of the subject.
2. To use the *self-pronoun* as the *object* of the verb and to impose the action of the subject on itself.

Observe the following sentences :

A. 1. I **myself** shall do it.
   2. The queen **herself** came to see her. } They emphasize the action.
   3. The king **himself** killed the dacoit.

B. 1. While cutting the apple, I hurt **myself**.
   2. He blamed **himself** for this sin. } They reflect the action on the subject itself.
   3. We enjoyed **ourselves** very much in Paris.

A. Write eight chief *personal pronouns* :

....

....

B. Write eight pronouns ending in *self* :

....

....

C. Pick out the *personal pronoun* and write it in the blank :

Sentences	Personal Pronouns
1. How many sisters have you ?	....
2. She has done the right thing.	....
3. Let us go boating today.	....
4. This book is mine.	....
5. They are real brothers.	....
6. These socks are hers.	....
7. Don't tease the dog. It may bite you.	....
8. We must never tell lies.	....
9. You should carry on your work.	....

D. Each sentence has a *self-pronoun* in it. Sort it out and write it in the blank. Also write whether it is *emphatic* or *reflexive* :

Sentences	Self-pronouns	Kinds
1. I cursed myself for my folly.	....	....
2. We enjoyed ourselves a lot there.	....	....
3. The dog seated itself near the door.	....	....
4. The child fell over and hurt itself.	....	....
5. She herself made her bed.	....	....

6. I spoke to the king himself.
7. The dacoit shot himself dead.
8. The wall itself fell down.
9. The king himself praised me.
10. Never give yourself too much of importance.

E. Define —

(a) a *personal pronoun* :

....

....

(b) an *emphatic self-pronoun* :

....

....

(c) a *reflexive pronoun* :

....

....

F. Put a *suitable self-pronoun* in each blank :

1. They enjoyed .... very much in the capital.

2. The ailing man hanged .... from the ceiling fan.

3. I .... shall complete this job.

4. The queen .... cooked her food.

5. You must do something to save ....

6. God helps those who help ....

7. We must .... try to complete this tough job.

8. The pup fell off the roof and hurt ....

9. The baby cried .... hoarse out of hunger.

10. You .... are to blame for your troubles.

We have studied two kinds of pronouns in the previous chapter. In this chapter, we shall study two more kinds of pronouns. They are—

1. Interrogative Pronoun   2. Demonstrative Pronoun

INTERROGATIVE PRONOUN

Observe the following sentences :

1. **Who** is there at the door ?
2. **Whose** is that book ?
3. **What** do you want now ?
4. **Whom** were you talking to ?
5. **Who** is taller of the two sisters ?

Each sentence has a word in bold type. It is a *question word* that asks something about the noun for which it stands. So, it is an **interrogative pronoun.**

An *interrogative pronoun* **is a pronoun that asks a question about the noun which it stands for.**

DEMONSTRATIVE PRONOUN

Observe the following sentences :

1. What is **this** ?
2. **That** is quite certain.
3. **It** is hailing outside.
4. This pen is finer than **that**.
5. I like this cloth. **It** is so smooth.
6. She is an elderly lady. We should respect her as **such**.

Each sentence has a word in bold type. It points to the noun for which it stands. In other words, it *demonstrates* a certain noun. So, it is a **demonstrative pronoun.**

A *demonstrative pronoun* is a pronoun that stands for a noun and also points to it.
Some other common demonstrative pronouns are :

this	that	these	those	it	same
so	one	ones	either	neither	none

TEST YOURSELF

A. Define an *interrogative pronoun*. Write five common interrogative pronouns :

....

....

....

B. Define a *demonstrative pronoun*. Write ten common demonstrative pronouns :

....

....

....

....

C. Sort out the *interrogative pronoun* in each sentence and write it in the blank :

   1.   Who is there in the kitchen ?   ....

   2.   What makes you laugh like that ?   ....

   3.   Which of the two is the elder ?   ....

   4.   What ails you, my son ?   ....

   5.   Whose umbrella is this ?   ....

   6.   Whom are you looking for ?   ....

   7.   What do you mean after all ?   ....

   8.   Which of these do you like best ?   ....

   9.   What is your father ?   ....

  10.   Who has broken the window-pane ?   ....

D. Sort out the *demonstrative pronoun* in each sentence and write it in the blank :

1. It is biting cold today. ....
2. It is really pleasant to hear this news. ....
3. This cloth is much finer than that. ....
4. You can take either of these shirts. ....
5. Is he a pick-pocket ? Yes, he is so. ....
6. Her frock is red but mine is a yellow one. ....
7. She looks so polite but her behaviour is not as such. ....
8. There are four yellow marbles and four blue ones. ....
9. Here comes two girls—one slim and the other fat. ....
10. Either of us must go for his help. ....

E. Underline the *pronoun* in each sentence and name its type in the blank :

1. I like this shirt. Which one will you buy ? ....
2. Look at the baby. How lovely it looks ! ....
3. This is not going to happen at all. ....
4. Which of them is your cousin ? ....
5. She likes blue ribbons, not red ones. ....
6. What is your uncle ? ....
7. He is our brother. We must love him as such. ....
8. She is more beautiful than her sister. ....
9. Play and fun are our basic needs. This refreshes .... the mind and that rejuvenates the body.

F. Put a suitable *interrogative pronoun* in each blank :

1. .... is there on the roof ?
2. .... is this fine frock ?
3. .... makes you weep so bitterly ?

4. .... did you come here for ?

5. .... did you abuse yesterday ?

6. .... of you can catch the thief ?

7. .... did you pay the money ?

8. .... is lying there behind the door ?

9. .... did you stay in Australia ?

10. .... do you do to earn your living ?

G. Put a suitable *demonstrative pronoun* in each blank :

1. .... is there in your left hand ?

2. .... is as certain as death.

3. China's population is larger than .... of Italy.

4. It is a serious problem. We must treat it as ....

5. Here comes two dogs — .... black and .... white.

6. My neck-tie is white but yours is a blue ....

7. Here are three round blocks and three square ....

8. I like this flower. .... is so fragrant.

9. .... is raining cats and dogs outside.

10. These dresses are far finer than ....

H. Use the following *pronouns* in your own sentences :

1. which : ....

2. either : ....

3. one : ....

4. whom : ....

5. those : ....

6. what : ....

7. such : ....

8. neither : ....

WHAT IS A SIMPLE SENTENCE ?

We read about the **sentence** in the previous book of this series. But sentences are of several types. One of these type is called the **simple sentence**. What is a *simple sentence* ?

A *simple sentence* **is a sentence with only one main verb ; as—**

1. The farmer **is ploughing** his field.
2. The labourers **are digging** the canal.
3. The girl **brushed** her hair with a comb.

Remember that if a sentence has more than one main verb, it is a **multiple sentence**.

TWO PARTS OF A SIMPLE SENTENCE

When a sentence is to be spoken or written, first of all, we think of a **noun** *that is the doer of an action or about which something is to be said.*

Then we think of a word that *expresses something about the above-stated noun.* This word is called **verb**.

Most of the words in the sentence centre round these two words. Let us read about these two words in detail.

SUBJECT

1. The **noun** that is the *doer of the action* is called the **subject**. It may have some words attached to it. For example—

(a) **Mac** is doing his homework.

(b) The three-legged **table** has a round top.

In (a) **Mac** is a single-word subject.

In (b) the subject consists of three words—**the three-legged table**. In these words, **table** is the real subject. The other two words—**the, three-legged** are the *enlargement of the subject.*

PREDICATE

The **verb** and the *words attached to it* are called **predicate.** This part of the sentence describes something about the subject. It may be an *action,* a *fact* or a *happening.* In the three sentences given above, the subject and the predicate are as follows :

No.	SUBJECT	PREDICATE
1.	The farmer	is ploughing his field
2.	The labourers	are digging the canal.
3.	The girl	brushed her hair with a comb.

So, we can define the *subject* and the *predicate* as under :

The *subject* of a sentence is a noun/pronoun that does the action stated in the sentence or about which something is said.

The *predicate* of a sentence expresses the action done by the subject or states a fact about it.

TEST YOURSELF

A. Sort out the *subject* and the *predicate* in each sentence and write them in the given blanks :

1. The farmer killed the snake with a stick.

   S : .... P : ....

2. The moon moves round the earth.

   S : .... P : ....

3. Alfred and Peter are fast friends.

   S : .... P : ....

4. The tailor-bird is building its nest in the tree.

   S : .... P : ....

5. Bread and butter is a perfect food.

   S : .... P : ....

6. Her younger brother scored two goals in only three minutes.

   S : .... P : ....

7. A kangroo's young-one is called a *joey*.

    S : .... P : ....

8. The lion is the king of the forest.

    S : .... P : ....

9. Only the brave deserve the best.

    S : .... P : ....

10. The tortoise moved slowly but steadily.

    S : .... P : ....

11. October is the tenth month of the year.

    S : .... P : ....

12. The teacher punished the late-comers severely.

    S : .... P : ....

13. The king has been holding his court for a long time.

    S : .... P : ....

14. The fisherman is sailing in the river for a good catch.

    S : .... P : ....

15. Our team has set a big target for the other team.

    S : .... P : ....

B. Put a *suitable subject* in each sentence :

1. .... is suffering from fever.

2. .... broke into the rich man's house.

3. .... will hold a meeting against the cat.

4. .... appears just above us in the sky.

5. .... helped the bee in time.

6. .... bring forth new leaves during spring.

7.   .... is sleeping soundly in the cradle.

8.   .... followed Mary to her school daily.

9.   .... bowled extremely well in this match.

10. .... contains very interesting stories in it.

C. Put a _suitable predicate_ in each blank :

1. Sincere friends ....

2. The shepherd ....

3. Good students ....

4. The milkman ....

5. The lark ....

6. Brave men ....

7. The queen ....

8. Women and watches ....

9. No other mountain ....

10. Paris ....

11. Our country ....

D. Define —

(a) a _simple sentence_ :

....

....

(b) a _subject_ :

....

....

(c) a _predicate_ :

....

....

We read about adjectives in the previous book. We know that adjectives are *describing words*. Each adjective adds something to the meaning of its noun. It describes any of its qualities.

Some adjectives are derived from **proper nouns**. Some other adjectives are used to **ask questions** about their own nouns.

Thus, we see that adjectives are of three main kinds as under :

1. Adjectives of Quality   2. Proper Adjectives   3. Interrogative Adjectives

Let us read about these three kinds of adjectives one by one.

ADJECTIVES OF QUALITY

Observe these sentences :

1. She has a **pink** *saree* on.
2. Bob is a **handsome** *lad*.
3. Alexander was a **great** *ruler*.
4. **Honest** *persons* are honoured everywhere.
5. **Charming** *girls* are taken as models.

Each sentence has a word in bold type. It mentions a *quality* of the noun that follows it. So, it is an **adjective of quality**.

An *adjective of quality* is an adjective that states a quality of its noun/pronoun.

PROPER ADJECTIVE

Observe these sentences :

American Color Program	British Colour Programme

1. **Chinese** *people* love peace.
2. This is a **Swiss** *watch*.
3. She is a **Canadian** *citizen*.
4. **American** *English* differs from British English.

Each sentence has a word in bold type. It has been derived from a *proper noun*. It acts as an adjective to the noun that follows it. So, it is a **proper adjective**.

A *proper adjective* is an adjective that is derived from a proper noun.

Given below is a list of some commonly used proper adjectives.

Proper Noun	Adjective	Proper Noun	Adjective
Persons			
Victoria	Victorian	Germany	German
Hercules	Herculean	America	American
Elizabeth	Elizabethan	Russia	Russian
George	Georgian	Japan	Japanese
Lands		Korea	Korean
Singapore	Singaporean	Nepal	Nepalese
Africa	African	Persia	Persian
Arabia	Arabian	Spain	Spanish
Asia	Asian	Turkey	Turkish
Britain	British	Europe	European
China	Chinese	France	French
Egypt	Egyptian	Italy	Italian
England	English	Austria	Austrian

INTERROGATIVE ADJECTIVES

Observe the following sentences :

1. **What** *colour* is the sky ?
2. **Which** *school* do you attend ?
3. **Whose** *pen* is this ?
4. **Which** *way* is the wind blowing ?
5. **Whose** *grandson* are you ?

Each sentence has a word in bold type. It is a *question word* and it acts as an adjective to the noun that follows it. So, it is an **interrogative adjective.**

An *interrogative adjective* is an adjective that precedes its noun and also asks a question about it.

☞ Remember that there are only three common interrogative adjectives— *what, which* and *whose.*

A. What is an *adjective* ? How many *kinds* of adjectives are there ? Name them.

....

....

B. What is an *adjective of quality* ? Give three examples.

....

....

C. What is a *proper adjective* ? Give three examples.

....

....

D. What is an *interrogative adjective* ? Give three examples.

....

....

....

E. Pick out the *adjective of quality* in each sentence and write it in the blank :

1. What a charming scenery it is !   ....
2. Pudding is my favourite dish.   ....
3. Diligent students get high marks.   ....
4. The lame tiger lay under a tree.   ....
5. Only brave men deserve the best.   ....
6. Oxen and he-buffaloes are farm animals.   ....
7. Young children are the citizens of tomorrow.   ....
8. Honest people are honoured everywhere.   ....
9. Ashley was the most charming queen.   ....
10. This book contains interesting stories.   ....

F. Pick out the *proper adjective* in each sentence and write it in the blank :

1. Thai cuisine is very delicious indeed. ....
2. Arabian people are famous for their hospitality. ....
3. British English is real English. ....
4. Chowmein is a Chinese dish. ....
5. Asian elephants are smaller than African elephants. ....
6. His wife works in a Japanese firm ....
7. American English is full of slang. ....
8. Swiss watches are considered to be the best. ....

G. Pick out the *interrogative adjective* in each sentence and write it in the blank :

1. Which flight did you come by ? ....
2. What kind of man are you ? ....
3. Whose pocket has been picked ? ....
4. Which movie are you going to see tonight ? ....

H. Pick out the *adjective* in each sentence. Write it in the blank and name its kind as well :

Sentences	Adjectives	Kinds
1. His wife is very faithful.	....	....
2. The rose is a beautiful flower.	....	....
3. What type of food do you like ?	....	....
4. Socrates was a great philosopher.	....	....
5. The Chinese alphabet has hundreds of letters.	....	....
6. The blind beggar stumbled and fell over.	....	....
7. William Shakespeare wrote many dramas.	....	....
8. Which dish do you like best ?	....	....

I. Use the following *adjectives* in sentences :

1. Australian : ....
2. patient : ....
3. charming : ....
4. cheerful : ....
5. which : ....
6. what : ....
7. Japanese : ....
8. English : ....

J. Put a *suitable adjective* in each blank :

1. The ....mother was waiting for her son.
2. Jennifer was a lady of .... beauty.
3. The .... Tales is a fine book of stories.
4. Our soldiers are the .... soldiers indeed.
5. The princess fell in love with a ....young man.
6. This shopkeeper is, in fact, very ....
7. ....colour are both her ribbons ?
8. .... shoes do you like—black or brown ?
9. Our country has produced very .... women as well.

K. Pick out *different adjectives* used in this passage and write them in the blanks :

The birthday of Jesus Christ is celebrated as Christmas on 25th December every year. The celebrations for Christmas start from Christmas Eve. At home, feasts are spreadout under a bedecked and illuminated Christmas tree. The Christmas luncheon is organised with meticulous care and special dishes are prepared. Santa Claus gives presents to children.

.... *(3 different adjectives)*

What is a *determiner* ?

A *determiner* is a small word that does two jobs :

(a) It *shows the reference in regard to the noun* that follows it.

(b) It *determines the limit of the meaning of that noun.*

The references made by determiners may be—

(a) *indefinite* : **a** man = *any man*

(b) *definite* : **the** man = *man mentioned earlier*

(c) *possessive* : **my** man = *somebody's man*

(d) *general* : **every** man = *all men*

(e) *particular* : **this** man = *a man pointed to*

(f) *numeral* : **some** men = *a few men*

(g) *quantitative* : **some** sugar = *a little sugar*

COUNTABLE AND UNCOUNTABLE NOUNS

In this lesson, we shall study the determiners **a, an.** But before that we must read about two categories of nouns—*countable* and *uncountable.*

Countable Noun. The nouns that can be counted are called *countable noun*; as: *boy, book, apple, animal* etc.

Uncountable Noun. The nouns that cannot be counted are called *uncountable noun*; as: *water, milk, sugar, wheat, tea* etc.

DETERMINERS A, AN

A and **an** have the same meaning-**one** or **any.** Both are used with countable singular nouns. But these nouns differ in one respect. Some countable singular nouns begin with *vowel-sounds* ; as : egg, ant, SM etc. Some countable singular nouns begin with *consonant sounds* ; as : *jug, slate, station master* etc.

USE OF A

The determiner—*a*—is used before the countable singular noun that begin with consonant sound ; as—

1. **A** *pen* is to write with.
2. Every sentence has **a** *verb*.
3. **A** *snake* caught **a** frog.
4. **A** *knife* is to cut with
5. I bought **a** new uniform.

In these sentences—

1. **A pen** means *any pen*.
2. **a verb** means *any verb*.
3. **a snake** means *any snake*.

   and **a frog** = *any frog*.
4. **A knife** = *any knife*.
5. **a uniform** = *any uniform*.

The following facts are clear from the above discussion :

1. **A** makes an *indefinite reference* to the nouns that follow it.
2. **A** is used before the countable singular noun that *begin with consonant sound*.
3. The word—**knife**—has its *k* silent. So, it begins with the consonant sound of *n*.
4. The word—**uniform**—starts with *u* which is a vowel but, in this word, it has its consonant sound similar to that of *y*.

USE OF AN

The determiner—*an*—is **used before the countable singular noun that begin with vowel sound ;** as—

1. This hen lays **an** *egg* daily.
2. Sixty minutes make **an** *hour*.
3. **An** *elephant* has a long trunk.
4. **An** *ant* and a dove became friends.
5. **An** *owl* is considered to be a wise bird.

In these sentences—

1. **An egg** means *any egg*.
2. **An hour** means *any complete hour*.
3. **An elephant** means *any elephant*.
4. **An ant** means *any ant*.
5. **An owl** means *any owl*.

The following facts are clear from the above discussion :

1. **An** makes an *indefinite reference* to the noun that follows it.
2. **An** is used before the countable singular noun that begin with vowel sound.
3. The word—**hour**—has its *h* silent. So, it begins with the vowel sound of *o*.

USING A, AN WITH ABBREVIATIONS

We must be very careful while using **a, an** with abbreviations. The reason is that the starting sound of some abbreviations become different from those of their full words. So, the use of *a, an* also becomes different accordingly. Here are some examples :

1. We say **a** *Station Master* but **an** *SM* (*ess, em*).
2. We say **a** *Lower Division Clerk* but **an** *LDC* (*el dee see*).
3. We say **a** *Forest Officer* but **an** *FO* (*ef o*).
4. We say **a** *Station House Officer* but **an** *SHO* (*ess ech o*).

ANOTHER IMPORTANT FACT

We often use *adjectives* before countable singular nouns. In such a case, the *sound starting the adjective* is taken into consideration for using **a, an** before them ; as—

1. **an** *easy* question 2. **a** *farm* animal 3. **a** *black* ant
4. **an** *early* bird   5. **an** *angry* man 6. **a** *white* elephant

To sum up, we must bear in mind *the following facts* regarding the use of **a, an** :

1. **A** and **an** are used before *countable singular nouns*.
2. **A** and **an** are *indefinite determiners* as they refer to nouns in an indefinite way.

3. **A** is used before those countable singular nouns that *start with any consonant sound.*

4. **An** is used before those countable singular nouns that *start with any vowel sound.*

5. When we use an adjective before a singular countable noun, the starting sound of the adjective decides the use of **a** and **an**.

6. We must use **a, an** with abbreviations very carefully. Their use with abbreviations often differs from that with full words.

TEST YOURSELF

A. **Here is a list of 10 common nouns. Five of them are** *countable* **and five** *uncountable.* **Write each noun in its column :**

| man | gold | pear | oil | wife |
| wheat | hill | tea | table | milk |

Countable : ....

Uncountable : ....

B. **Write** *a* **or** *an* **in each blank :**

(a) 1............... ape   2. .... tent   3. .... chair

4............... grocer   5. .... SP   6. .... orange

7............... uniform   8. .... injury   9. .... beggar

10............. MLA   11. .... UDC   12. .... LDC

13............. organ   14. .... verb   15. .... adverb

16............. pronoun 17. .... adjective 18. .... FIR

(b) 1............... easy question   2. .... flightless bird

3. .... one-eyed man   4. .... honest man

5. .... dishonest boy   6. .... eight-legged spider

7. .... useful machine   8. .... out-door game

9. .... indoor game   10. .... unpleasant climate

C. Change the nouns and pronouns in each sentence to their *singular forms* and then use *a* or *an* with them :

1. Eyes are very sensitive organs.

....

2. Ripe tomatoes are blood-red in colour.

....

3. Watches help us to be regular and punctual.

....

4. Banyan trees are very huge trees.

....

5. Tables are made of wood or steel.

....

6. Honest people are respected everywhere.

....

7. Houses provide us with comfort, safety and unity.

....

8. Silent dogs are believed to be dangerous.

....

9. Bears can be white, brown or black.

....

10. Soldiers are generally brave and disciplined.

....

D. Define —

(a) a countable noun   :   ....

(b) an uncountable noun   :   ....

(c) an indefinite determiner :   ....

F. In the following passage, *a* or *an* has been omitted in every line. Rewrite the passage supplying *a/an* where necessary :

Once upon time, there was Greek   ....
king and he had son called Paris.   ....
Troy was ancient country where   ....
king Priam rulled it.   ....

As mentioned in the previous chapter, **the** is a *definite determiner* since it refers to a noun that has become **definite** in one way or the other. Given below are the chief rules for using the determiner **the** :

A. *The* is used before unique natural objects :

the earth   the sky

the equator   the north pole

the sun   the moon

the tropic of cancer

B. *The* is used before a singular common noun that stands for its entire class :

1. **The** *lion* is the king of animals.
2. **The** *dog* is a faithful pet.
3. **The** *giraffe* is the tallest animal.
4. **The** *whale* is the largest sea-animal.

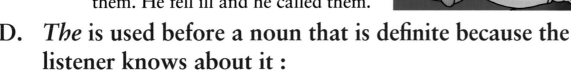

C. *The* is used before a noun when it has become definite by repetition :

1. Once there lived an old farmer. **The** farmer had three sons. **The** sons were lazy and good-for-nothing fellows. **The** old farmer was worried about them. He fell ill and he called them.

D. *The* is used before a noun that is definite because the listener knows about it :

1. Switch on **the** light, please.
2. Turn off **the** tap. **The** water is running unnecessarily.
3. Switch **the** cooler on ; it is very hot.

E. *The* is used before adjectives to make them plural universal nouns :

1. **The** poor must be helped.
2. **The** good are always blessed.
3. **The** wicked has to suffer in the long run.
4. **The** dead are burnt or buried.

F. *The* is used before ordinal numbers used as determiners :

1. I am a student of **the** *4th* grade.
2. **The** *first* boy in **the** *second* row is my son.
3. It is **the** *15th* of May, today.
4. He got **the** *third* prize in the competition.

G. *The* is used before the superlative degree of adjectives :

1. Mary is **the** *tallest* of all the three sisters.
2. Asia is **the** *largest* continent.
3. Alexander was **the** *greatest* of all **the** rulers.
4. Australia is **the** *smallest* continent.

H. *The* is used before the words—morning, evening, afternoon :

1. The sun rises in **the** *morning* and sets in **the** *evening*.
2. We take tea in **the** *afternoon*.

I. *The* is used before the names of—

(a)	**seas** and **oceans**	: the *Pacific Ocean*, **the** *Red Sea*
(b)	**rivers**	: the *Thames*, **the** *Nile*
(c)	**mountain ranges**	: the *Rockys*, **the** *Andes*
(d)	**island groups**	: the *West Indies*, **the** *East Indies*
(e)	**trains**	: the *Orient Express*, **the** *Summit Express*
(f)	**books** and **magazines**	: the *Quran*, **the** *Bible*
(g)	**newspapers**	: the *Dawn*, **the** *New York Times*
(h)	**communities**	: the *Muslims*, **the** *Christians*

Where we don't use—the

1. We never write **the** before the names of **lakes** and **mountain-peaks** : *Superior Lake, Mount Everest.*

2. Students and teachers never use *the* before the word **school** :

   (a) I go to school.   *(b) Teachers come to school to teach.*

TEST YOURSELF

A. Write *a, an* or *the* in each blank :

1. .... uniform
2. .... engine
3. .... East Indies
4. ....inn-keeper
5. .... book-rack
6. .... Bible
7. .... polar bear
8. .... Thames
9. .... elf
10. .... unit
11. .... eel
12. .... Black Sea
13. .... coward
14. ....animal
15. .... Pacific Ocean

B. Put *a, an* or *the* in each blank to complete the sentence :

1. .... horse is .... very faithful animal.
2. This is quite .... easy sum. I can solve it now.
3. ....earth is ....unique planet of .... solar system.
4. Where there is .... will, there is .... way.
5. What .... charming scenery it is indeed !
6. ....coward dies many times before .... actual death.
7. I am going to have .... X-ray of my right lung.
8. ....sky is ....endless empty space about .... earth.
9. Who does not know that 60 minutes make .... hour ?
10. ....Muslims pray in mosques but ....Christians in churches.

C. Rewrite each sentence after inserting a *determiner* where needed :

1. I saw tiger, lion and elephant in zoo.

   ....

2. Tropic of Cancer lies 23½° north of equator.

   ....

3. I first met her year ago.

   ....

4. He is most courageous man I have ever seen.

   ....

5. Mount Everest is highest mountain-peak in world.

   ....

6. My father came to school to see my principal.

   ....

7. Aeroplanes flies in sky.

   ....

8. Roses are loveliest of all flowers.

   ....

9. Pigeons flew away in sky along with net.

   ....

10. It is said that fear is biggest sin.

    ....

D. Answer the following :

1. Before which three natural objects is **the** used ?

   ....

2. Which degree of adjectives takes **the** before it ?

   ....

3. When does a common noun become **definite** ?

   ....

4. Make *ordinals* from :

   one ....   two ....   six ....

5. When does a common noun *stand for its entire group* ?

....

6. Before which noun do students not use *the* ?

....

E. Remove the *determiner* — *the* — where it is not needed :

1. The student reached the school on time.

....

2. The Mount Everest is the highest mountain-peak.

....

3. Daddy leaves for the office at 7-00 a.m. every day.

....

4. Many students come to the school on the foot.

....

5. The English is popular all the world over.

....

6. A horse and a carriage is at the door.

....

7. The natural beauty needs no ornaments at all.

....

8. The sun is just overhead at the noon.

....

F. In the following passage, *the* has been left off at several places. Write the passage again putting *the* where ever necessary :

One day a tortoise was walking along road. On his way, he met a hare. Hare laughted at him and said, "Isn't it sad that you can't move fast ?" Tortoise was upset at this. Tortoise challenged hare to participate in a running race. Finally, tortoise won in race.

....

....

....

....

....

In this lesson, we shall study numeral determiners. They are—

no	some	any	many	more
most	both	either	neither	every
each	all	one	first	twice

1. NO

No = *not any* ; as—

1. There is **no** *book* in the bag.
2. She has **no** *friends* here.
3. He is **no** *player* to speak of.
4. The match-box has **no** *sticks* in it.

2. SOME

Some = *a few*. It has a *positive sense* ; as—

1. The basket has **some** *mangoes*.
2. I must come to see you **some** *day*.
3. **Some** *fool* has broken my slate.
4. **Some** *girls* are dancing there.

3. ANY

Any = *one* or *some but no matter which*. It has a *negative sense* ; as—

1. **Any** *person* can do it.
2. Are there **any** *apples* in the basket ?
3. Did you see **any** *children* there ?
4. **Any** *food* is welcome for a saint.

MANY, MORE, MOST

(a) **Many** = *more than one* ; as—

1. **Many** *people* do not believe in God.

2. I have **many** *friends* but Peter is the best of them.

3. I have already warned you **many** *times* against this danger.

(b) **More** = *more than in hand* ; as—

1. **More** *workers* are needed to finish this job.

2. Here are some **more** *examples* of it.

3. We need to buy **more** *computers*.

(c) **Most** = *a majority of* ; as—

1. **Most** *people* are selfish by nature.

2. **Most** *children* are fond of sweets.

3. **Most** *girls* are shy and modest.

BOTH, EITHER, NEITHER

(a) **Both** = *the one* and also *the other* ; as—

1. **Both** *brothers* are intelligent.

2. I held the ball with **both** *hands*.

3. **Both** *ends* of the rope are worn out.

(b) **Either** = *the one* or *the other* ; as—

1. **Either** *side* of the street has a police-post.

2. **Either** *side* of the road has shady trees.

(c) **Neither** = *not the one* and *not the other* ; as—

1. **Neither** *end* of the street has a gate.

2. **Neither** *computer* is in working order.

3. **Neither** *candidate* is suitable.

ALL, EACH, EVERY

(a) **All** = *one and all* ; as—

1. **All** *men* are not equal.

2. **All** the *children* are eating chocolates.

3. We are **all** *brothers* and sisters.

(b) **Each** = *taken one by one* (singular sense, singular verb).

1. **Each** *player* has his own bat.

2. **Each** *shop* has a similar board.

3. **Each** *soldier* has his own gun.

(c) **Every** = *applicable to each one*
(plural sense but singular verb).

1. **Every** *living-being* breathes air in and out.

2. **Every** *child* has a scarf.

3. **Every** *town* has a municipality.

ONE, FIRST, TWICE

(a) **One** = *a/an, single*

1. **One** *person* cannot make a group.

2. **One** *year* is a long period for it.

3. **One** *day* is enough for this job.

(b) **First** = *No 1 in order*

1. January is the **first** *month* of the year.

2. I'll see you in the **first** *week* of June.

3. The **first** *boy* of this row is my son.

(c) **Twice** = *two times*

1. **Twice** *5* is equal to ten.

2. **Twice** *it* will be sufficient.

TEST YOURSELF

A. **Each sentence has a *numeral determiner*. Sort it out and write in the blank :**

Sentences	*Determiners*
1. Either room is fairly large.	....
2. I bought some mangoes from the fruitseller.	....
3. Is there any pen in the drawer ?	....
4. Each winner was praised highly.	....
5. Most people are greedy by nature.	....

6. Neither restaurant is clean and tidy. ....
7. One sheet is enough for me. ....
8. Sunday is the first day of the week. ....
9. All animals depend on plants for food. ....
10. Cats have no horns on their heads. ....
11. Every man has to die sooner or later. ....
12. Either kettle is made of steel. ....

B. Use each of these *numeral determiners* in a sentence :

1. few : ....
2. no : ....
3. more : ....
4. most : ....
5. some : ....
6. any : ....
7. neither : ....
8. either : ....
9. some : ....
10. third : ....
11. every : ....
12. all : ....

C. Fill up each blank :

1. The determiner **some** has a ....sense.
2. The determiner **any** has a ....sense.
3. **All** = ...
4. **Both** = ...
5. **Either** = ...
6. The determiner **every** has a .... sense.
7. The determiner **each** has a .... sense.

8. **Neither** = ...

9. **No** = ...

10. **Second** = ...

D. Put a suitable *determiner* in each blank :

It was .... hot summer noon. I was sitting in .... drawing-room. I had a book in .... hands. I was reading .... story from .... book. The story had .... fine character. Suddenly I heard .... loud noise. .... people were running in .... direction. .... man had .... stick. I came to .... gate of our house and banged it with .... hands. .... fool had bolted it from outside.

E. Fill up each blank with a *numeral determiner* :

1. .... man wants to have a charming wife.

2. .... end of our street has an iron-gate.

3. .... blind men came to see ....elephant.

4. .... worker was given Rs. 500 as .... award.

5. .... wrestlers are fair, tall and hefty.

6. .... people are objecting to the new rules.

7. Our house has .... big lawn and .... gates.

8. The .... month of the year is called March.

9. The .... letter of the English alphabet is Z.

10. .... steps were taken to improve our knowledge.

11. As many as .... people were sitting there.

12. .... queens and their ....maids came to the church to pray.

We have studied numeral determiners in the previous chapter. In this chapter we shall read about determiners that refer to the quantities of their nouns. Such words of quantity are as under :

    (a)   some, any, no, all   *(b)*   much, more, most   *(c)*   little, less, least

    (d)   whole, half, part   *(e)*   enough, such, certain

Let us read about these determiners in detail.

A. SOME, ANY, NO, ALL

    (a)   SOME

Some is used both as a *numeral* and a *quantitative* determiner. It has a positive sense and means a **small amount** ; as—

1. We need **some** *time* to take a decision.
2. Bring **some** *wood* to make a fire.
3. There may be **some** *truth* in your words.
4. **Some** *gain* must come out of it.

    (b)   ANY

Any is also used both as a *numeral* and a *quantitative* determiner. It has a *negative sense* and it is generally used in negative and interrogative sentences. It means *some but no matter which* ; as—.

1. You may come to see me **any** *time*.
2. I do not need **any** *help* from you.
3. It won't make **any** *difference* to me.
4. Is there **any** *sugar* in the house ?

    (c)   NO

No has a totally *negative sense*. It is also used both as a *numeral* and a *quantitative* determiner. It means **not any** ; as—

1. It is **no** *use* crying over spilt milk.
2. I need **no** *help* from anybody.
3. There is **no** *milk* in the jug.
4. No pain, **no** *gain*.

(d) ALL

All = *the entire amount*. It is also used as a *numeral* and as a *quantitative* determiner ; as—

1. **All** *work* and no play makes one dull.
2. **All** *pollution* is due to smoke and petrol fumes.
3. **All** *grief* is due to undue desires.
4. **All** *responsibility* is on my shoulders.

B. MUCH, MORE, MOST

(a) MUCH

Much = *a lot of* ; as—

1. **Much** *effort* is needed to achieve it.
2. An empty vessel makes **much** *noise*.
3. Markets have **much** *rush* on holidays.
4. I still need **much** *money* for this project.

(b) MORE

More = *a larger amount* ; as—

1. I can give you **more** *information* on this topic.
2. **More** *effort* is required to achieve it.
3. **More** *sugar* is needed for the sweets.
4. Do you need **more** *help* from me ?
5. It is sure to put **more** *strain* on your mind.

(c) MOST

Most = *a still larger amount* ; as—

1. **Most** *noise* is due to loud-speakers.
2. **Most** *pollution* is due to smoke and fumes.
3. **Most** *grief* is because of undue desires.

C. LITTLE, LESS, LEAST

(a) LITTLE

Little has a *negative sense* and it means *almost no* ; as—

1. We have **little** *hope* of his recovery.

2. He gave us **little** *help* during our bad times.
3. **Little** *pain*, **little** *gain*.
4. She has **little** *courage* to oppose the injustice.

(b) LESS, LESSER

Less = *a smaller amount* ; as—
1. We can do more work in **less** *time* using a machine.
2. The labourers are paid **less** *wages* everywhere.
3. **Less** *work* brings in **less** *money*.
4. **Less** *input* leads to **less** *output*.

Lesser = *less* but it is used in general statements ; as—
1. We must choose the **lesser** *evil* of the two.
2. Crops like maize flourish in **lesser** *rainfall*.
3. **Lesser** *responsibility* should be given to him.

(c) LEAST

Least = *very small amount* ; as—
1. She paid **least** *attention* to my requests.
2. This machine needs the **least** *amount* of energy to be worked.
3. **Least** *pain* brings in **least** *gain*.

D. WHOLE, HALF, PART

(a) WHOLE

Whole = *an undivided singular thing* ; as—
1. I have bought a **whole** *bread*.
2. You have spoiled the **whole** *plan*.
3. The **whole** *scheme* is foolish.
4. I spent the **whole** *year* away from home.

(b) HALF

Half = *one of the two equal parts of a thing* ; as—
1. Can you eat a **half** *chicken* at a time ?
2. Never do anything with a **half** *mind*.
3. A **half** *kilogram* is equal to 500 grams.
4. **Half** *satisfaction* is no satisfaction.

(c)   PART

Part = *any part of a thing* ; as—

1. I am not ready to accept a **part** *payment*.
2. His job is **part** *time* so far.
3. **Part** *force* applied to the wheel will not move it.

E.   ENOUGH, SUCH, CERTAIN

(a)   ENOUGH

Enough = *a good lot/sufficient* ; as—

1. We have bought **enough** *wheat* for the whole year.
2. You have spent **enough** *energy* on it.
3. This job needs **enough** *time* to be completed.

(b)   SUCH

Such = *of this type* ; as—

1. **Such** *music* does not appeal to the ear.
2. **Such** *noise* is sure to make me deaf.
3. Can you brook **such** *non-sense* ?

(c)   CERTAIN

Certain = *a particular amount* ; as—

1. **Certain** *patience* is needed to handle this situation.
2. I can say it with **certain** *confidence*.
3. A **certain** *amount* of force is needed to move this log.

TEST YOURSELF

A.   Sort out the *quantitative determiner* and write it in the blank :

Sentences	Determiners
1. I heard some noise in the street.	....
2. No help can rid us of this trouble.	....
3. All play and no work makes one lazy.	....

4. Do you need any help from me ? ....
5. I have earned enough money in life. ....
6. If you must, choose the lesser evil. ....
7. Less work cannot bring more gain. ....
8. Her charm deserves much praise. ....
9. He has made little improvement indeed. ....
10. This job requires a certain amount of labour. ....

B. Use the following as *numeral* as well as *quantitative* determiners :

1. all : *(a)* ....
   (b) ....
2. no : *(a)* ....
   (b) ....
3. any : *(a)* ....
   (b) ....
4. some : *(a)* ....
   (b) ....
5. more : *(a)* ....
   (b) ....

C. Use as directed :

1. *an* as a numeral determiner :

   ....

2. *no* as a numeral determiner :

   ....

3. *all* as a quantitative determiner :

   ....

4. *any* as a quantitative determiner.

   ....

5. *some* as a numeral determiner :

   ....

6. *lesser* as a quantitative determiner.

....

7. *most* as a numeral determiner.

....

8. *any* as a numeral determiner.

....

9. *certain* as a quantitative determiner.

....

10. *neither* as a numeral determiner.

....

D. Put a suitable *quantitative determiner* in each blank :

1. I have .... money to last my ....life.
2. .... milk, sugar and tea-leaves are needed to make tea.
3. .... pollution is there due to noise and smoke.
4. .... money invested in this scheme will be wasted.
5. This labour will not bear .... fruit, my child.
6. Spread ....jam on this slice of bread and eat it.
7. You need to pay ....attention to this serious problem.
8. We have ....right to destroy a thing which we cannot make.
9. I am not going to accept .... payment at all.
10. You are not going to do .... more work.

E. Sort out *different determiners* in this passage and write them below :

All religions lead to one and the same goal. Each religion was simple to start with. But gradually evil practices went on creeping into it. It happened because of some people who were not very sincere towards the religion they followed. They were in no mood to follow the good principles. So, they urged people for some foul practices for their good. Nature never pardons such people. Theyhad to suffer many punishments and undergo much grief in life.

....
....

(10 different determiners)

We know the following facts about verbs.

1. The **verb** of a sentence is its *very soul*.

2. **Verbs** state *something about nouns* or *pronouns*.

3. All the *following words* revolve round the **verb :**

    (a) the word used for the *doer of the action*.

    (b) the word for the *noun whom the action affects*.

    (c) the word naming the *instrument of the doer's action*.

    (d) the word naming the *time, place* or *manner* of the action.

    (e) the word stating the *cause/purpose of the action*.

    (f) the word stating the *result of the action*.

WHAT IS A VERB ?

Observe the following sentences :

1. The earth **is** round in shape.   *(fact)*
2. It **is raining** very heavily.   *(happening)*
3. Alice **is singing** a sweet song.   *(action)*

In these sentences—

1. **is** affirms *a fact* about the earth.
2. **is raining** expresses a *natural happening*.
3. **is singing** expresses an *action done by Alice*.

So, we see that each sentence has a word/words in bold type. Each of these words either *affirms a fact* or *states a happening* or *expresses an action*. Such words are called **verbs**.

A *verb* is a word that affirms a fact, states a happening or expresses an action.

HELPING VERBS AND MAIN VERBS

Observe the following sentences :

1. He **brushes** his teeth after every meal.
2. It *is* **raining** very heavily.

3. Girls *are* **singing** a sweet song.

4. I *am* **doing** my homework now.

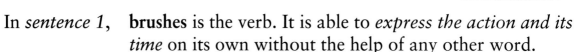

In the above sentences—

In *sentence 1,* **brushes** is the verb. It is able to *express the action and its time* on its own without the help of any other word.

In *sentence 2,* **rain** is the *main verb.* But it seeks the help of the word **is** to express the *action* and its *manner.*

In *sentence 3,* **sing** is the *main verb.* But it seeks the help of the word **are** to express the *action* and its *quality.*

In *sentence 4,* **do** is the *main verb.* But it seeks the help of the word **am** to express the *action* and its *time.*

The words that help the main verbs to express their actions etc. are called **helping** or **auxiliary** verbs. But the words that can express actions on their own are called **main** or **principal** verbs.

A *principal (main) verb* is a word that can express an action or a fact/ happening singly, *i.e.* without the help of any other word.

An *auxiliary/helping verb* is a word that is used to help a main verb in expressing an action or a fact/happening.

THREE OTHER KINDS OF VERBS

As for *actions* stated by verbs, they fall into three classes :

1. An action *limited to the doer (subject) only.*

2. An action that *affects another noun/pronoun also.*

3. An action that *affects two other nouns/pronouns also.*

On the basis of these three types of actions, verbs also fall into three classes— *Transitive, Ditransitive* and *Intransitive.*

1. TRANSITIVE VERB

Transitive—means *that transits* or *passes on.* So, it is clear that—

a *transitive verb* is a verb that passes on the action of the doer to some other noun or pronoun ; as—

1. **I** wrote a *letter.*

2. **The** *farmer* **killed** the *snake.*

3. *Mummy* **cooked** a *sweet dish.*

In these sentences—

1. The **action of writing** passes on to the *letter.*
2. The **action of killing** passes on to the *snake.*
3. The **action of cooking** passes on to the *dish.*

Remember that the noun/pronoun to which the action of a subject passes is called the OBJECT.

2. DITRANSITIVE VERB

A *ditransitive verb* **is a verb that passes on the action of the doer to two objects ; as—**

1. I **gave** my *bat* to *him.*
2. He **sent** *me* a *present.*
3. The teacher **taught** *us* a *lesson.*

In these sentences—

1. The **action of giving** has gone to the *bat* and to *him.*
2. The **action of sending** has gone to *me* and to the *present.*
3. The **action of teaching** has gone to *us* and to the *lesson.*

The *two objects* in each of the above sentences consist of a **thing** and a **person.** Remember that—

(a) the thing is called the DIRECT OBJECT ; as—

   bat, present, lesson.

(b) the person is called the INDIRECT OBJECT ; as—

   him, me, us.

3. INTRANSITIVE VERB

An *intransitive verb* **is the verb that does not pass on the action of the doer to any object ; as—**

1. I **rise** very early in the morning.
2. A hare **can** run very fast.
3. Most plants **grow** wild.
4. The baby is **sleeping** very soundly.

In these sentences—

1. The **action of rising** *ends* with the subject *I.*
2. The **action of running** *ends* with the subject *hare.*
3. The **action of growing** *ends* with the subject *plants.*
4. The **action of sleeping** *ends* with the subject *baby.*

Remember that a verb that does not pass on the doer's action is called an **intransitive verb.**

One more thing is to be remembered that there are verbs that are used both *transitively* and *intransitively.*

Given below are some common verbs used both *intransitively* and *transitively* :

Intransitive	Transitive
1. Hares **run** very fast.	1. She is **running** a *school.*
2. The sun **sets** in the evening.	2. You must **set** an *example.*
3. His leg *has* **broken.**	3. He **has broken** his *leg.*
4. It is **blowing** very hard.	4. The referee **blew** a *whistle.*
5. Sugar **tastes** sweet.	5. Just **taste** this *dish.*
6. The clock **struck** ten.	6. I **struck** *him* with a rod.
7. Birds **fly** in the air.	7. The boys **fly** kites.
8. The lamp is **burning.**	8. **Burn** the *lamp* at once.
9. Most plants **grow** wild.	9. Farmers **grow** *crops.*
10. The church-bell is **ringing.**	10. The peon is **ringing** the *bell.*
11. A tortoise **moves** slowly.	11. **Move** this *stone* away.
12. The mouse **stole** into its hole.	12. The mouse **stole** food.

TEST YOURSELF

A. Pick out *auxiliary* and *principal* verbs and write them in their blanks :

1. Mummy is cooking a sweet dish for the guests.

   Auxiliary .... *Principal* ....

2. I have scored three field-goals in this match.

   Auxiliary .... *Principal* ....

3. The frog was hopping about in the compound.
   Auxiliary .... *Principal*................................

4. Have you completed your home-work carefully ?
   Auxiliary .... *Principal*................................

5. Our school starts at 8 o'clock in the morning.
   Auxiliary .... *Principal*................................

B. Underline the *verb* in each sentence. Write in the blank whether it is *transitive, intransitive* or *ditransitive* :

Sentences	Verbs
1. The peon is ringing the bell.	....
2. The candle is burning.	....
3. *I wrote a letter to him.*	....
4. *The toad hopped about in the compound.*	....
5. *My uncle sent me a present.*	....
6. *All living-beings keep growing.*	....
7. *The teacher taught us a new lesson.*	....
8. *She offered me a cup of tea.*	....

C. Define —

(a) a *verb* :

....

....

(b) an *intransitive verb* :

....

....

(c) a *transitive verb* :

....

....

(d) a *distransitive verb* :

....

....

(e)   *the subject of a sentence :*

....

(f)   the *object* of a *sentence :*

....

D. Write a *transitive verb* in each blank :

1. Ask the labourer to .... this heavy log.
2. The thieves ....into the house of the landlord.
3. Our captain ....three field-goals in the match.
4. The lion .... the tiny mouse in its big paw.
5. The dove .... a dry leaf near the drowning bee.
6. The general .... his men to march forward.

E. Write an *intransitive verb* in each blank :

1. A lark loves to ....high in the cooler air.
2. Cloth ....by the metre and sugar by the kilogram.
3. Most plants .... wild after heavy rains.
4. The wall-clock .... just ....ten.
5. A cobra .... fast raising its head above the ground.
6. The widow .... bitterly to see her only son dead.

F. Sort out the *objects* in each sentence and write which is the *direct object* and which is the *indirect* one :

1. I have paid him his salary.
   Direct ....   Indirect ....
2. The queen rewarded her maid a gold necklace.
   Direct ....   Indirect ....
3. The juggler showed us wonderful feats.
   Direct ....   Indirect ....
4. The father left his children a huge property.
   Direct ....   Indirect ....
5. Grandpa sent his love for all the children.
   Direct ....   Indirect ....

We have read about *transitive, intransitive* and *ditransitive* verbs. Also, we have learnt what *helping* and *main* verbs are. The main verbs have different forms when used to express actions done in the **three different periods of time** and to be used with different **persons, numbers, tenses** and **voices**. So, each main verb has three forms as under :

1. **The First Form** : It is used for actions done in the present time (*time going on*). It is also called the **base form.**

2. **The Second Form** : It is used for actions done in the past period of time (*time gone by*). It is also called **past form.**

3. **The Third Form** : It is used for actions that were completed in the present or in the past period of time. It is also called the **past participle form.**

Needless to say, we must learn the three forms of the most commonly used verbs in order to be able to speak and write English correctly. These three forms of verbs are called their **conjugation.**

CONJUGATION OF VERBS

	Present	*Past*	*Past Participle*
A.	arise	arose	arisen
	awake	awoke	awoken
	bear	bore	born/borne
	beat	beat	beaten
	become	became	become
	begin	began	begun
	bind	bound	bound
	bite	bit	bitten
	blow	blew	blown
	break	broke	broken
	catch	caught	caught
	choose	chose	chosen
	come	came	come

Present	Past	Past Participle
dig	dug	dug
do	did	done
drink	drank	drunk
drive	drove	driven
eat	ate	eaten
fall	fell	fallen
feed	fed	fed
fight	fought	fought
find	found	found
fly	flew	flown
forget	forgot	forgotten
get	got	got
give	gave	given
go	went	gone
grow	grew	grown
have/has	had	had
hear	heard	heard
keep	kept	kept
know	knew	known
lay	laid	laid
lead	led	led
leave	left	left
learn	learnt	learnt
lend	lent	lent
lie	lay	lain
light	lighted/lit	lighted/lit
lose	lost	lost
make	made	made
mean	meant	meant
meet	met	met

Present	Past	Past Participle
pay	paid	paid
ride	rode	ridden
ring	rang	rung
rise	rose	risen
run	ran	run
say	said	said
see	saw	seen
send	sent	sent
shake	shook	shaken
sing	sang	sung
sink	sank	sunk
sit	sat	sat
sleep	slept	slept
smell	smelt	smelt
speak	spoke	spoken
spend	spent	spent
stand	stood	stood
steal	stole	stolen
swim	swam	swum
take	took	taken
tear	tore	torn
teach	taught	taught
think	thought	thought
throw	threw	thrown
weave	wove	woven
weep	wept	wept
win	won	won
write	wrote	written

B. **The following verbs have all the *three forms alike* :**

bid	burst	cast	cost	cut	hit	hurt	let
put	read	rid	set	shed	shut	split	spread

C. These verbs add *d* to make their *second* and *third* forms :

agree	arrive	care	die	divide
dance	dare	manage	prove	state
taste	tease	vote	waste	yoke

D. These verbs add *ed* to make their *second* and *third* forms :

bow	drown	earn	enter
hunt	kill	kiss	pass
push	pray	roam	stay
touch	roll	watch	guard

THE VERB—TO BE

Remember that **be** is a very commonly used verb. It is used as a principal verb and also as an auxiliary verb. Its forms are as follows :

Present	*Past*	*Past Participle*
is, am, are	was, were	been

Be is used as a *principal verb* to express **facts** : as—

1. Tom **is** a carpenter.   2. Gold **is** a costly metal.
3. The girl **was** tall, slim and extremely fair.

Be is used as an *auxiliary verb* with other **main verbs** ; as—

1. The carpenter **is** making a table.
2. Eddie **was** dressing her hair.
3. He **was** imprisoned for six months.
4. I **am** to go to America tomorrow.

TEST YOURSELF

A. Write the *three forms* of each of the following verbs :

wake	....	bite	....
fight	....	leave	....
pay	....	sell	....

teach	....	....	hear	....	....
have	....	....	say	....	....
lay	....	....	take	....	....
shake	....	....	give	....	....
bind	....	....	fly	....	....
do	....	....	beat	....	....
lie	....	....	drive	....	....
lose	....	....	fly	....	....

B. Write —

(a) the three forms of the verb—*be*—in the present tense.

....

(b) two forms of the verb—*be*—in the past form.

....

(c) two sentences in which—*be*—is used as a principal verb.

1. ....

2. ....

(d) two sentences in which—*be*—is used as a helping verb.

1. ....

2. ....

(e) ten verbs that have all their *three forms* alike.

....

....

(f) fifteen verbs that form their *second* and *third* forms by adding *d*.

....

....

....

(g) fifteen verbs that form their *second* and *third* forms by adding *ed*.

....

....

....

C. Here are five pictures. Three of them belong to the *present time*, one to the *past time* and one to the *future time*. Write three sentences for each of them :

1. ....
2. ....
3. ....

1. ....
2. ....
3. ....

May 2007

1 2 3 4 5 6 7
8 9 10 11 12 13 14
15 16 17 18 19 20 21
22 23 24 25 26 27 28
29 30 31

1. ....
2. ....
3. ....

1. ....
2. ....
3. ....

January

1 2 3 4 5 6 7
8 9 10 11 12 13 14
15 16 17 18 19 20 21
22 23 24 25 26 27 28
29 30 31

2010

1. ....
2. ....
3. ....

We know that—**it**—is a pronoun. But we use it in an **impersonal** way also to start sentences that have no relation with any person. Such sentences contain general and impersonal information that is useful to *any* and *every* person. We use it as under :

A. TO EXPRESS TIME

1. **It** will be *Sunday* tomorrow.
2. **It** is *nightfall*.
3. **It** is *afternoon*.
4. **It** is *the third period*.
5. **It** is *Friday* today.
6. **It** is *quite late*.
7. **It** is *the month of June*.
8. **It** is *morning*.
9. **It** is *too early*.
10. **It** is *the 7th of July* today.
11. **It** is *time for tea*.
12. **It** is *7-15 a.m.*

B. TO EXPRESS WEATHER

1. **It** is *quite pleasant* today.
2. **It** was *hot* and *stuffy* yesterday.
3. **It** was *biting cold* last night.
4. **It** is *mostly cloudy* in July.
5. **It** looks *like rain* today.
6. **It** was *awfully windy* yesterday.
7. **It** may be *sunny* tomorrow.
8. **It** was *calm and sunny* on Sunday.
9. **It** is *raining* cats and dogs.
10. **It** is also *hailing* outside.
11. **It** is *snowy* on high mountains.
12. **It** is *cosy and warm* inside.

C. TO REFER TO PERSONS

1. Who is **it** at the door ?
2. **It** is me, sir, James.
3. **It** is he who has done it.
4. **It** is we who are to blame.
5. **It** was Alex who beat me.
6. **It** was they who helped us.

D. TO EXPRESS IMPERSONAL INFORMATION

1. **It** is silly to think like that.
2. **It** was quite shameful on your part.
3. **It** is said that honesty is the best policy.
4. **It** is well known that he is a pick-pocket.
5. **It** was foolish of us to trust him.

6. **It** is no use crying over spilt milk.

7. **It** is no use waiting for him any longer.

8. **It** is highly necessary to be ready for it.

9. **It** is likely that such a thing will happen.

10. **It** is not essential at all.

11. **It** was foolish of you to annoy him.

NEGATIVE FORM

In order to change a sentence with *introductory it* into its **negative form, not** is inserted after **is, was** or **will** ; as—

	Positive	*Negative*
1.	It **is** biting cold today.	It **isn't** biting cold today.
2.	It **was** Friday yesterday.	It **wasn't** Friday yesterday.
3.	It **will be** wise of you to do so.	It **won't be** wise of you to do so.

INTERROGATIVE FORM

In order to change a sentence with *introductory it* into its **interrogative form**, we shift **is, was** or **will** of the positive form to the beginning of the sentence ; as—

	Positive	*Interrogative*
1.	It **is** biting cold today.	**Is** it biting cold today ?
2.	It **was** Friday yesterday.	**Was** it Friday yesterday ?
3.	It **will be** wise of you to do so.	**Will** it **be** wise of you to do so ?

NEGATIVE-INTERROGATIVE FORM

In order to change a sentence with *introductory it* into its **negative-interrogative form,** we shift **isn't, wasn't** or **won't** of the *negative form* to the beginning of the sentence ; as—

	Negative	*Negative-Interrogative*
1.	It **isn't** biting cold today.	**Isn't** it biting cold today ?
2.	It **wasn't** Friday yesterday.	**Wasn't** it Friday yesterday ?
3.	It **won't be** wise of you to do so.	**Won't** it be wise of you to do so?

A. **Supply the correct form of—*it is*—in each blank :**

1. .... scorchingly hot the day before yesterday.
2. .... silly of you to waste money like that.
3. .... strange that she also happened to be there ?
4. .... 9th of March when I got married.
5. .... really shameful if you behave like that.
6. .... widely believed that good deeds bring in joy.
7. .... no use at all to spend money on it.
8. .... not likely that such a thing will ever happen.

B. **Answer the following :**

1. How is the weather today ?   ....
2. What time is it by your watch ?   ....
3. What date is it today ?   ....
4. Which period is it ?   ....
5. Which month is it ?   ....
6. Will it be wise to say so ?   ....
7. Which time of the day was it ?   ....
8. What date was it on that day ?   ....

C. **Change each sentence to its *negative* and *interrogative* form :**

1. It is no use repenting of the folly now.
   Neg. ....
   Int. ....
2. It is time to have some refreshment.
   Neg. ....
   Int. ....
3. It is funny to be dressed like that.
   Neg. ....
   Int. ....

There is an *adverb*. But it is also used to *introduce sentences* in all the tenses. That is why it is called **introductory** *there*. Mostly it is used to state something that *exists* or *does not exist* at some place. This use of *there* is **impersonal** just like that of *it*. *There* is also used in some expressions. Let us study the use of *introductory there* in detail.

A. TO SHOW EXISTENCE

1. **There** is an egg on the plate.
2. **There** is someone inside the room.
3. **There** must be something wrong in the matter.
4. **There** was once a church at this place.
5. **There** is a box lying there.

Remember that in the above sentences, *there* is not the subject. The *subject* of the sentence is the noun that follows *is, am, are, must, was* etc.

Also, remember that another *there* can be used as an adverb if needed. The *introductory* **there** has nothing to do with the **there** used as an adverb. Both of them must never be confused ; as : *There is* a cap lying **there.**

B. TO SHOW INEXISTENCE

1. **There** *isn't* any egg on the plate.
2. **There** *isn't* anyone at the door.
3. **There** should not be a repetition of this error.
4. **There** was never any church at this place.
5. **There** is not any cup on the table.

C. IN SOME EXPRESSIONS

1. **There is no hope** of her recovery.
2. **There is no doubt** that Richard Hadlee was the best all-rounder of his time.
3. **There is no reason** to feel worried.
4. **There is no point** in spending anything on it.

D. IN CONDITIONAL SENTENCES

1. If rabbits are not **there**, foxes and wolves will attack grazing sheep.

2. If smoke is there, a fire must also be there somewhere around.

3. If children are there, their noise is a must.

NEGATIVE AND INTERROGATIVE FORMS

Positive

(a) There is a cup on the table. ⎤ There is no cup on the table.
There is not any cup on the table.
⎦ *(Negative)*

(b) There is a girl in the ball-room. ⎤ Is there any girl in the ball-room ?
⎦ *(Interrogative)*

(c) There was a tree behind the hut. ⎤ Isn't there any girl in the ball-room?
⎦ *(Interrogative-Negative)*

TEST YOURSELF

A. Write the correct form of *there is* in each blank :

1. .... is a fountain in the park.

2. .... once a mosque at this place.

3. .... any pen in the drawer ?

4. .... a primary school in every village.

5. .... any other train for London ?

6. .... no post-office in this small town ?

7. It is a pity that .... no school here.

8. .... a special drink for every guest at the party ?

83

B. Each sentence starts with *there*. Rewrite it beginning with *it* :

1. There is no doubt that he is the best batsman.

   ....

2. There is no wisdom in spending money on it.

   ....

3. There is no hope of her recovery.

   ....

4. There is no possibility of doing it.

   ....

5. There is no likelihood that he will come.

   ....

C. Each sentence starts with *it*. Rewrite it beginning with *there* :

1. It is not likely that she will come here.

   ....

2. It is pointless to feel worried.

   ....

3. It is no use hoping for his recovery.

   ....

4. It is silly to be disappointed.

   ....

5. Is it wise to behave like this ?

   ....

D. Supply the correct form of *there is/it is* for each blank :

1. .... very pleasant the day before yesterday.

2. If smoke .... , a fire must also be there.

3. ....a pity that she did not greet you.

4. ....a beautiful park near my office.

5. ....too early to say anything about it.

The word—**tense**—means *stretched*. In grammar, this word means—*a stretch of time, i.e.* **a period.** There are three chief periods of time as under :

1. The period of time *that is going on*   = **present period.**
2. The period of time *that has passed*   = **past period.**
3. The period of time *that is yet to come*   = **future period.**

Clearly, there are three main tenses :

1. The Present Tense   2. The Past Tense   3. The Future Tense

In order to know the tense of a sentence, we have to see which of these three periods of time, its action/fact/happening belong to.

Observe the following sentences :

1. Bill Clinton was the president of United States.   *(past tense)*
2. George Bush is the president of United States.   *(present time)*
3. Mr X **will be** our next president.   *(future tense)*

The word—**was**—is the *past form* of the verb **be.**
The word—**is**—is the *present form* of the verb **be.**
The word—**will be**—is the *future form* of the verb **be.**

THE PRESENT TENSE

The *present tense* is the period (stretch) of time which is going on and which lies between the *period that has passed* and the *period that is yet to come.*

THE PAST TENSE

The *past tense* is the period (stretch) of time that has *passed before the present period.*

THE FUTURE TENSE

The *future tense* is the period (stretch) of time that is *yet to come after the present period.*

Each tense has four **sub-kinds.** These sub-kinds are based on three factors :

(a) **Time** of the *action/fact/happening.*

(b) **Continuity** of the *action/fact/happening.*

(c) **Completeness** of the *action/fact/happening.*

As each tense has four sub-kinds, there are 12 tenses in all as under :

(a) INDEFINITE TENSE

It has its present, past and future forms. Verbs in this tense **do not indicate any definite time** of the actions/facts/happenings in all its three forms.

(b) CONTINUOUS TENSE

It has its present, past and future forms. Verbs in this tense indicate the **continuity** of the actions/facts/happenings in all its three forms.

(c) PERFECT TENSE

It has its present, past and future forms. Verbs in this tense indicate the **completeness** of the actions/facts/happenings in all its three forms.

(d) PERFECT CONTINUOUS TENSE

As the name shows, this tense is a combination of **continuous** and **perfect tenses.** Verbs in this tense show both *completeness* and *continuity* of the actions/facts/happenings in all its three forms.

We shall study six out of the twelve tenses in this book. They are—

1. Present Indefinite Tense	2. Present Continuous Tense
3. Past Indefinite Tense	4. Past Continuous Tense
5. Future Indefinite Tense	6. Future Continuous Tense

TEST YOURSELF

A. Answer the following :

(a) What does the word—*tense*—mean ?

....

(b) How many main periods of time are there ?

....

(c)   What is meant by the *present tense* ?

....

....

(d)   What is meant by the *past tense* ?

....

....

(e)   What is meant by the *future tense* ?

....

(f)   How many forms does each tense have ?

....

(g)   How many tenses are there in all ?

....

B.   Name —

(a)   three factors on which the kinds of tenses are based :

....

(b)   the factor that the *three definite tenses* do not indicate :

....

(c)   the factor that the *three continuous tenses* indicate :

....

(d)   the factor that the *three perfect tenses* indicate :

....

(e)   the two factors that the *three perfect continuous tenses* indicate :

....

C.   Which tense does each sentence belong to ?

                                       Present tense

1.   The earth revolves round the sun.   ....
2.   Our team wins almost every match ruler.   ....
3.   The 21st century will be the age of computers.   ....
4.   I play football daily.   ....
5.   Mary sings a song every night ?   ....
6.   Who rang the bell ?   ....
7.   I am doing my homework.

We read about the *Indefinite Tense* in the previous chapter. The present form of this tense is called **Present Indefinite Tense**. It is also called **Simple Present Tense**.

This tense is used to express two types of actions etc. in the present tense :

1. *Actions that are done as habits almost daily.*   **Habitual Actions**
2. *Simple actions done in the present time.*   **Simple Actions**

This tense expresses these two types of actions. But it *does not indicate their definite time*. It simply states that they are done in the present period of time. So, this tense is called **Present Indefinite Tense**. Let us see how this tense is formed.

POSITIVE FORM

The **positive form** of the *present indefinite tense* is formed by using the **base form** (first form) **of the verb** after the subject. But if the *subject is singular* and of *the third person* (he, she, it), we add **s** or **es** *to the verb* ; as—

I **do** my homework.	*But*	*He* **does** his homework.
We **do** our homework.		*She* **does** her homework.
They **do** their homework.		*John* **does** his homework.

INTERROGATIVE FORM

The **interrogative form** of the *present indefinite tense* is formed by adding **do/does** in *the beginning* of the sentence ; as—

Do I *do* my homework ?	*But*	**Does** he *do* his homework ?
Do we *do* our homework ?		**Does** she *do* her homework ?
Do they *do* their homework ?		**Does** John *do* his homework ?

☞ 1. Remember that when we use **does,** the **s/es** of the base form of the verb is removed.

2. In the sentences starting with question-words (*who, when, where, why* etc.), these words *are followed by interrogative sentences.*

NEGATIVE FORM

The **negative form** of the *present indefinite tense* is formed by adding **do not** or **does not** before the *base form of the verb* ; as—

I **do not** *do* my homework.	*But*	He **does not** *do* his homework.
We **do not** *do our* homework.		She **does not** *do* her homework.
They **do not** *do* their homework.		John **does not** *do* his homework.

INTERROGATIVE-NEGATIVE FORM

The **interrogative-negative form** of the *present indefinite tense* is formed by **shifting do/does** of *the negative form* to the **beginning** of the sentence ; as—

Do I **not** *do* my homework ?	*But*	**Does** he **not** *do* his homework ?
Do we **not** *do* our homework ?		**Does** she **not** *do* her homework ?
Do they **not** *do* their homework ?		**Does** John **not** *do* his homework ?

TEST YOURSELF

A. **Fill up each blank with the *present indefinite form* of the verb given in brackets :**

1. We ....hockey in the evening daily. *(play)*
2. It ....very hard in the afternoon. *(blow)*
3. I ....to God daily in the morning. *(pray)*
4. My mother .... me ready for school every day. *(get)*
5. My father .... in an office in London. *(work)*
6. She .... very sweet songs in the evening. *(sing)*
7. He ....to the library for books every day. *(go)*
8. You ....exercise regularly in the morning. *(take)*
9. The children .... story-books in the library. *(read)*
10. They ....to the movies every Sunday. *(go)*

B. Change each sentence into its *interrogative* and *negative* forms :

1. Mummy cooks food for us all.

   Int. ....

   Neg. ....

2. The watchman guards our houses at night.

   Int. ....

   Neg. ....

3. Every father earns money for his family.

   Int. ....

   Neg. ....

4. Good children obey their parents and teachers.

   Int. ....

   Neg. ....

5. Birds fly to their nests after sunset.

   Int. ....

   Neg. ....

6. I never laugh at the poor and the needy.

   Int. ....

   Neg. ....

7. The teacher calls the roll in the morning.

   Int. ....

   Neg. ....

8. The baby cries loudly in hunger.

   Int. ....

   Neg. ....

C. Read the example and use each given word into a sentence in the *present indefinite tense* :

Example : *Why* **do you weep** so bitterly ?

Now use the following question words in your sentences :

1. when : ....
2. why : ....
3. what : ....
4. where : ....
5. who : ....
6. whose : ....

D. Use each of the following verbs in the *present indefinite form* :

1. weep : ....
2. write : ....
3. dance : ....
4. sleep : ....
5. sweep : ....

E. Answer the following :

(a) Which two types of actions does *present indefinite tense* express ?

1. .... 2. ....

(b) How is the *positive form* of the present indefinite tense formed ?

....

(c) How is the *negative form* of the present indefinite tense formed ?

....

(d) How is the *interrogative form* of the present indefinite tense formed ?

....

(e) How is the *interrogative-negative form* of the present indefinite tense formed?

....

The *present continuous tense* shows actions *that are going on now*. So, it is called **Real Present Tense** also. Let us see how this tense is formed.

POSITIVE FORM

The **positive form** of the *present continuous tense* is formed by using **is/am/are + first form of the verb + ing** after the *subject* ; as—

I **am doing** my homework.   He **is doing** his homework.

We **are doing** our homework.   She **is doing** her homework.

They **are doing** their homework.   John **is doing** his homework.

INTERROGATIVE FORM

The **interrogative form** of the *present continuous tense* is formed by **shifting is/am/are** *of the positive form* to the **beginning** of the sentence ; as—

Am I *doing* my homework ?   **Is** he *doing* his homework ?

Are we *doing* our homework ?   **Is** she *doing* her homework ?

Are they *doing* their homework ? **Is** John *doing* his homework ?

NEGATIVE FORM

The **negative form** of the *present continuous tense* is formed by inserting **not** between *is/am/are* and the *main verb* of the sentence ; as—

I **am not** *doing* my homework.   He is **not doing** *his* homework.

We **are not** *doing* our homework. She **is not** *doing* her homework.

They **are not** *doing* their homework. John **is not** *doing* his homework.

INTERROGATIVE-NEGATIVE FORM

The **interrogative-negative form** of this tense is formed by **shifting is, am, are** *of the negative form* to the **beginning** of the sentence ; as—

Am I **not** *doing* my homework ?   **Is** he **not** *doing* his homework?

Are we **not** *doing* our homework ?   **Is** she **not** *doing* her homework ?

Are they *not doing* their homework ?   **Is** John **not** *doing* his homework ?

TEST YOURSELF

A. **Fill up each blank with the *present continuous form* of the verb given in brackets :**

1. The black bear .... up the tree slowly.   *(climb)*
2. The labourers .... at the heavy log.   *(heave)*
3. The elephant ....a log in its trunk.   *(lift)*
4. The hounds .... the hare.   *(chase)*
5. The stag ....his thin legs again and again.   *(curse)*
6. The peon .... the prayer-bell on time.   *(ring)*
7. Someone .... at the door. Go and open it.   *(knock)*
8. We ....a test in English today.   *(take)*
9. The baby .... bitterly in hunger.   *(cry)*

B. **Use the *present continuous form* of each of the following verbs in a sentence of your own :**

1. hear   : ....
2. tell   : ....
3. boast   : ....
4. roar   : ....
5. tremble : ....

C. **Change each sentence into its *interrogative* and *negative* forms :**

1. The gardener is weeding and watering the plants.

   Int. ....

   Neg....

2. The watchman is sitting on a stool at the gate.

Int. ....

Neg. ....

3. She is preparing very diligently for the coming test.

Int. ....

Neg. ....

4. The thieves are breaking into the house.

Int. ....

Neg. ....

5. They are having a stroll in the park.

Int. ....

Neg. ....

6. The birds are flying to their nests.

Int. ....

Neg. ....

7. People are basking in the warm sun.

Int. ....

Neg. ....

8. The hounds are chasing the stag.

Int. ....

Neg. ....

D. Write a sentence in the *present continuous tense* starting with each of the following question-words :

1. who   : ....

2. whose : ....

3. whom : ....

4. when   : ....

5. where : ....

E. Change into *interrogative-negative* form :

   1. Four ducks are swimming in the pool.

       ....

   2. The robbers are distributing the loot among themselves.

       ....

   3. Two cocks are fighting fiercely.

       ....

   4. The soldiers are marching to the battlefield.

       ....

F. Answer the following :

   1. What does the *present continuous tense* express ?

       ....

       ....

   2. What is the other name for the *present continuous tense* ?

       ....

       ....

   3. How is the *positive form* of the present continuous tense formed ?

       ....

       ....

   4. How is the *negative form* of the present continuous tense formed ?

       ....

       ....

   5. How is the *interrogative form* of the present continuous tense formed ?

       ....

       ....

   6. How is the *interrogative-negative form* of this tense formed ?

       ....

       ....

The **first form** of the verb is used to form the *present indefinite tense*. Clearly, we use the **second form** of the verb to form **Past Indefinite Tense**.

POSITIVE FORM

The **positive form** of the *past indefinite tense* is formed by using the **second form** of the verb after each and every subject ; as—

I **did** my homework.

We **did** our homework.

They **did** their homework.

He **did** his homework.

She **did** her homework.

John **did** his homework.

INTERROGATIVE FORM

The **interrogative form** of the *past indefinite tense* is formed by adding **did** in the **beginning** of the sentence and **changing** *the verb from its second form to the first form* ; as—

Did I *do* my homework ?

Did we *do* our homework ?

Did they *do* their homework ?

Did he *do* his homework ?

Did she *do* her homework ?

Did John *do* his homework ?

NEGATIVE FORM

The **negative form** of the *past indefinite tense* is formed by **adding did not** between the *subject* and the *main* verb of the sentence ; as—

I **did not** *do* my homework.

We **did not** *do* our homework.

They **did not** *do* their homework.

He **did not** *do* his homework.

She **did not** *do* her homework.

John **did not** *do* his homework.

INTERROGATIVE-NEGATIVE FORM

The **interrogative-negative** form of the *past indefinite tense* is formed by **shifting** the **did** *of the negative form* to the **beginning** of the sentence ; as—

Did I **not** *do* my homework ?

Did he **not** *do* his homework ?

| Did we **not** *do* our homework ? | Did she **not** *do* her homework ? |
| Did they not *do* their homework ? | Did John **not** *do* his homework ? |

TEST YOURSELF

A. **Fill up each blank with the *past indefinite form* of the verb given in brackets :**

1. Bob and Mary .... carom on Sunday. *(play)*
2. It ....very, very hard on that day. *(blow)*
3. She ....very hard at her studies. *(work)*
4. The boys ....a treasure box. *(find)*
5. The morning bell ....at 8-30 a.m. today. *(ring)*
6. The cook .... a sweet dish for the guests. *(prepare)*
7. The American soldiers ....the enemy back. *(fight)*
8. The children ....sweets from their mother. *(demand)*
9. The frogs .... aloud in the tank. *(croak)*
10. The mother-crow ....two eggs in its nest. *(lay)*

B. **Use each of the following verbs in their *past indefinite forms* in your own sentences :**

1. wear : ....
2. plough : ....
3. graze : ....
4. thank : ....
5. shout : ....

C. **Change each sentence to its *interrogative* and *negative* forms :**

1. The wind blew very hard all through the night.

   Int. ....

   Neg. ....

2. The meeting broke up at 6-00 p.m.

Int. ....

Neg. ....

3. Children played hide and seek in the house.

Int. ....

Neg. ....

4. Michael told a white lie before the teacher.

Int. ....

Neg. ....

5. Rains broke out in the first week of July.

Int. ....

Neg. ....

6. The jackals howled loudly in the forest.

Int. ....

Neg. ....

7. The milkman brought milk for us every day.

Int. ....

Neg. ....

8. The Betty dried her long hair in the warm sun.

Int. ....

Neg. ....

9. We enjoyed ourselves a lot at the picnic.

Int. ....

Neg. ....

D. Change each sentence into its *interrogative-negative* form :

(a) We had great fun at the picnic.

....

(b) The post man cleared the letter box.

....

(c) The shepherd shouted loudly for help.

....

(d) The teacher taught a new lesson today.

....

(e) The host entertained his guests duly.

....

E. **Use the following *question-words* in sentences of your own :**

who : ....

what : ....

how : ....

why : ....

where : ....

whose : ....

whom : ....

which : ....

F. **Answer the following :**

1. How is the *positive form* of the past indefinite tense formed ?

....

2. How is the *interrogative form* of the past indefinite tense formed ?

....

3. How is the *negative form* of the past indefinite tense formed ?

....

4. How is the *interrogative-negative form* of the past indefinite tense formed ?

....

The **Past Continuous Tense** expresses actions that *were continuously done in the time gone by*. Let us see how this tense is formed.

POSITIVE FORM

The *positive form* of the *past continuous tense* is formed by using **was/were + first form of the verb + ing** after the subject ; as—

I **was doing** my homework.   He **was doing** his homework.
We **were doing** our homework.   She **was doing** her homework.
They **were doing** their homework.   John **was doing** its homework.

INTERROGATIVE FORM

The **interrogative form** of the *past continuous tense* is formed by **shifting was/were** of the positive form to the **beginning** of the sentence ; as—

Was I *doing* my homework ?   **Was** he *doing* his homework ?
Were we *doing* our homework ?   **Was** she *doing* her homework ?
Were they *doing* their homework ?   **Was** John *doing* its homework ?

NEGATIVE FORM

The **negative form** of the *past continuous tense* is formed by inserting **not** between the *subject* and the *ing-verb* ; as—

I *was* **not** *doing* my homework.   He *was* **not** *doing* his homework.
We *were* **not** *doing* our homework.   She *was* **not** *doing* her homework.
They *were* **not** *doing* their homework.   John *was* **not** *doing* his homework.

INTERROGATIVE-NEGATIVE FORM

The **interrogative form** of the *past continuous tense* is formed by **shifting was/were** of the *negative form* to the **beginning** of the sentence ; as—

Was I **not** *doing* my homework ?   **Was** he **not** *doing* his homework?

Were we **not** *doing* our homework ?   **Was** she **not** *doing* her homework ?
Were they **not** *doing* their homework ? **Was** Pat **not** *doing* his homework ?

TEST YOURSELF

A. **Fill up each blank with the *past continuous form* of the verb given in brackets :**

1. My friends .... me in every way.   *(help)*
2. The labourers .... the canal in the hot sun.   *(dig)*
3. The snake-charmer .... his feats.   *(show)*
4. I ....highly indisposed.   *(feel)*
5. The kites ....very high in the sky.   *(fly)*
6. The tailor-bird ....its nest.   *(build)*
7. Jackals .... in the class-room.   *(howl)*
8. The old men .... in the sun on the roof.   *(bask)*
9. The children .... cricket in the park.   *(play)*
10. The king .... at the head of a large army.   *(march)*

B. **Use *past continuous forms* of the following verbs in your own sentences :**

1. reap   : ....
2. creep   : ....
3. shiver : ....
4. prepare : ....
5. chase   : ....

C. **Change each sentence into its *interrogative* and *negative* forms :**

1. Ashley's mother was washing her school uniform.
   Int. ....
   Neg. ....

2. We all were doing our homework.

   Int. ....

   Neg. ....

3. Katy was sleeping in the class room.

   Int. ....

   Neg. ....

4. The widow was looking for her son.

   Int. ....

   Neg. ....

5. The old man was walking with the help of a stick.

   Int. ....

   Neg. ....

6. The principal was giving away the prizes.

   Int. ....

   Neg. ....

7. The farmers were ploughing their fields.

   Int. ....

   Neg. ....

8. The dog was barking at the stranger.

   Int. ....

   Neg. ....

9. The cobra was running fast towards its hole.

   Int. ....

   Neg. ....

10. People were running after the thief.

    Int. ....

    Neg. ....

D. Change each sentence into its *interrogative-negative* forms :

1. We were having a walk in the moonlight.

   ....

2. The policeman was beating the thief.

   ....

3. The lark was singing cheerfully in the sky.

   ....

4. My mother was cooking food in the kitchen.

   ....

E. Use the following question-words to start sentences in the *past continuous tense* :

1. who : ....
2. whom : ....
3. where : ....
4. why : ....
5. what : ....
6. which : ....
7. how : ....

F. Answer the following :

1. How is the *positive form* of the past continuous tense formed ?

   ....

2. How is the *interrogative form* of the past continuous tense formed ?

   ....

3. How is the *negative form* of the past continuous tense formed ?

   ....

4. How is the *interrogative-negative form* of the past continuous tense formed ?

   ....

We have learnt in the earlier lesson that the **future tense** indicates the *stretch of time* that is yet to come. In this lesson, we shall study the **Future Indefinite Tense**. It is also called **Simple Future Tense**.

The *future indefinite tense* expresses simple actions to be done in the time to come. Let us see how this tense is formed.

POSITIVE FORM

The **positive form** of the *simple future tense* is formed by using **shall** or **will** *before the base form* of the verb ; as—

I **shall** *do* my homework.	He **will** *do* his homework.
We **shall** *do* our homework.	She **will** *do* her homework.
They **will** *do* their homework.	John **will** *do* his homework.

☞ Remember that we use **shall** with *I* and *we* only. With all other subjects, we use **will**.

INTERROGATIVE FORM

The **interrogative form** of the *present indefinite tense* is formed by **shifting shall/will** to the **beginning** of the sentence ; as—

Shall I *do* my homework ?	**Will** he *do* his homework ?
Shall we *do* our homework ?	**Will** she *do* her homework ?
Will they *do* their homework ?	**Will** John *do* his homework ?

NEGATIVE FORM

The **negative form** of the *future indefinite tense* is formed by using **not** between *shall/will* and the *main verb* ; as—

I *shall* **not** *do* my homework.	He *will* **not** *do* his homework.
We *shall* **not** *do* our homework.	She *will* **not** *do* her homework.
They *will* **not** *do* their homework.	John *will* **not** *do* his homework.

INTERROGATIVE-NEGATIVE FORM

The **interrogative-negative form** of the *future indefinite tense* is formed by **shifting will/shall** of the negative form to the **beginning** of the sentence ; as—

Shall I **not** *do* my homework ?   **Will** he **not** *do* his homework ?

Shall we **not** *do* our homework ?   **Will** she **not** *do* her homework ?

Will they **not** *do* their homework ?   **Will** John **not** *do* his homework ?

TEST YOURSELF

A. **Fill up each blank with the *future indefinite form* of the verb given in brackets :**

1. The teacher ....us a test in English tomorrow.   *(give)*
2. Birds .... to their nests soon after sunset.   *(fly)*
3. We .... in the park tomorrow morning.   *(jog)*
4. The sun ....at 5-30 a.m. tomorrow.   *(rise)*
5. The train .... the station on time.   *(reach)*
6. The crowd ....the police-station in the evening.   *(attack)*
7. He ....up to be a very handsome lad.   *(grow)*
8. They .... us in every way in this task.   *(help)*
9. First of all I ....my homework.   *(do)*
10. She .... a fine sweet dish for us all.   *(cook)*

B. *Use the future indefinite form of each of the following verbs in a sentence of your own :*

1. sell   :..
2. march   : ....
3. wait   : ....
4. hang   : ....
5. guard   : ....

C. Change each sentence to its *interrogative* and *negative* forms :

1. The tiger will kill the bait and run away.

   Int. ....

   Neg. ....

2. They will land in serious trouble before long.

   Int. ....

   Neg. ....

3. I shall stay at home all day long.

   Int. ....

   Neg. ....

4. The train will reach the station on time.

   Int. ....

   Neg. ....

5. My uncle will send me a present on my birthday.

   Int. ....

   Neg. ....

6. They will sell all their property and go to London.

   Int. ....

   Neg. ....

7. She will act as the heroine of this film.

   Int. ....

   Neg. ....

8. The birds will build nests for the summer season.

   Int. ....

   Neg. ....

D. Make a sentence with *future indefinite tense* starting with each of the following question-words :

1. what   : ....
2. why   : ....
3. where   : ....
4. when   : ....
5. whose   : ....

E. Answer the following :

1. What is the other name for the *future indefinite tense* ?

....

2. How is the *positive form* of the future indefinite tense formed ?

....

3. How is the *negative form* of the future indefinite tense formed ?

....

4. How is the *interrogative form* of the future indefinite tense formed ?

....

F. Change each sentence into its *interrogative-negatgive form* :

1. Our soldiers will defeat the enemy before long.

....

2. The hare and the tortoise will have a race.

....

3. The peon will ring the bell at 8-50 a.m.

....

4. Our school will remain closed for two months.

....

5. Our English teacher will teach us a new lesson tomorrow.

....

The **Future Continuous Tense** is used to express *actions* or *happenings* that seem quite sure to happen in the time to come. It may be because of *circumstances* or because of *some arrangement* that has been made ; as—

1. We **shall be taking** a test in English tomorrow.
2. I **shall be doing** my homework at that time.
3. It **will be snowing** hard at midnight.

Let us study how this tense is formed.

POSITIVE FORM

The **positive form** of the *future continuous tense* is formed by using **shall be** or **will be + ing-form of the verb** after the *subject* ; as—

I **shall be** *doing* my homework.   He **will be** *doing* his homework.
We **shall be** *doing* our homework.   She **will be** *doing* her homework.
They **will be** *doing* their homework.   John **will be** *doing* his homework.

INTERROGATIVE FORM

The **interrogative form** of the *future continuous tense* is formed by **shifting shall/will** *of the positive form* to the **beginning** of the sentence ; as—

Shall I *be doing* my homework ?   **Will** he *be doing* his homework ?
Shall we *be doing* our homework ?   **Will** she *be doing* her homework ?
Will they *be doing* their homework ?   **Will** John *be doing* its homework ?

NEGATIVE FORM

The **negative form** of the *future continuous tense* is formed by inserting **not** between *shall/will* and the *main verb* of the positive form ; as—

I *shall* **not** be *doing* my homework.   He *will* **not** be *doing* his homework.
We *shall* **not** be *doing* our homework.   She *will* **not** be *doing* her homework.
They *will* **not** be *doing* their homework.   John *will* **not** be *doing* his homework.

INTERROGATIVE-NEGATIVE FORM

The **interrogative-negative form** of the *future continuous tense* is formed by **shifting will/shall** of the negative form to the **beginning** of the sentence ; as—

Shall I **not** be *doing* my homework ?   **Will** he **not** be *doing* his homework ?

Shall we **not** be *doing* our homework ?   **Will** she **not** be *doing* her homework ?

Will they **not** be *doing* their homework ?   **Will** John **not** be *doing* his homework ?

TEST YOURSELF

A. **Fill up each blank with the *future continuous form* of the verb given in brackets :**

1. The teacher .... us a test in English tomorrow.   *(give)*
2. The children ....a chorus on the stage.   *(sing)*
3. The girls .... in the ball-room.   *(dance)*
4. The lady ....her hair before the mirror.   *(comb)*
5. We ....for you outside the gate.   *(wait)*
6. Richard ....from high fever then.   *(suffer)*
7. I .... my birthday-party at that time.   *(hold)*
8. The old widow ....for his dead son.   *(weep)*
9. The people .... at the sky in wonder.   *(look)*

B. Use the following verbs in the *future continuous tense* :

1. blow   : ....
2. rain   : ....
3. do   : ....
4. *have*   : ....
5. fly   : ....
6. attend   : ....
7. reap   : ....

C. *Write questions in* future continuous tense *starting with these words :*

1. what : ....
2. which : ....
3. where : ....
4. who : ....
5. whose : ....

D. *Change each sentence to its* interrogative *and* negative *forms :*

1. It will be raining cats and dogs then.

   Int. ....

   Neg. ....

2. Trees will be bringing forth new leaves in March.

   Int. ....

   Neg. ....

3. We shall be celebrating Mac's birthday on Sunday.

   Int. ....

   Neg. ....

4. The court will be announcing its judgement on Monday.

   Int. ....

   Neg. ....

5. The postman will be delivering mail at mid-day.

   Int. ....

   Neg. ....

6. They will be leaving for London by month-end.

   Int. ....

   Neg. ....

7. The teacher will be getting angry with me for my rudeness.

   Int. ....

   Neg. ....

8. The bee will be stinging the hunter at his right hand.

   Int. ....

   Neg. ....

9. Mummy will be cooking a sweet dish for all of us.

   Int. ....

   Neg. ....

E. Change each sentence into its *interrogative-negative forms* :

1. My friends will be helping me in trouble.

   ....

2. Misty will be boasting of her figure and beauty.

   ....

3. I shall be solving sums at that time.

   ....

4. John will be smoking a cigarette in the park.

   ....

F. Answer the following :

1. Which actions are expressed in the *future continuous tense* ?

   ....

2. How is the *positive form* of this tense formed ?

   ....

3. How is the *interrogative form* of this tense formed ?

   ....

4. How is the *negative form* of this tense formed ?

   ....

I. NOUNS

A. ALWAYS PLURAL

alms	goods	scissors
ashes	jeans	shears
cattle	manners	shorts
clothes	pants	thanks
compasses	people	tongs
dividers	police	trousers
gentry	riches	wages

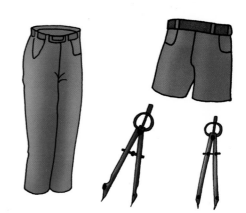

B. ALWAYS SINGULAR

advice	furniture	news
alphabet	hair	rice
army	innings	physics
cloth	luggage	plastics
crockery	mathematics	politics
crowd	milk	scenery
family	money	wheat

C. COMMON ERRORS IN THE USE OF NOUNS

1. The teacher writes with a **piece of chalk**.   (not *a chalk*)
2. My grandpa gave me **much advice**.   (not *many advices*)
3. Eddie gave me **much abuse**.   (not *many abuses*)
4. Her father deals in **cloth**.   (not *clothes*)
5. There is no **room** for you on the sofa.   (not *place*)
6. Children learn the **alphabet** first of all.   (not *alphabets*)
7. All the **members of my family** are educated.   (not *family members*)

II. PRONOUNS

A. WHO, WHAT, WHICH

(a) **Who** is always used *for persons* ; as—

Who is she ? **Who** is *your* English teacher ? Who goes there?

(b) **What** is always used for *things* ; as—
What is this ? **What** made you weep ?

(c) **Which** is used for *persons* as well as *things* for selection ; as—
Which book do you like more ?
Which is your favourite movie ?

B. COMMON ERRORS IN THE USE OF PRONOUNS

1. **You** and **I** are classmates.	(not *I* and *you*)
2. **You, he** and **I** shall go boating.	(not *I, you* and *he*)
3. **One** must keep **one's** promise.	(not *his* or *her*)
4. My pen is superior to **Peter's.**	(not Peter)

III. DETERMINERS

1.	**A black and white** cow *is* grazing.	(not *cows*, not *are*)
2.	**A black** and **white** cows *are* grazing.	(not *cow*, not *is*)
3.	**Rice** and **curry** *is* a perfect food.	(not *are*)
4.	**A horse and carriage** *is* at the gate.	(not *are*)
5.	**A horse** and **a carriage** *are* at the door.	(not *is*)

IV. ADJECTIVES

A. BITTER

1. a *bitter* enemy = sworn 2. a *bitter* fight = fierce
3. a *bitter* experience = lesson-giving 4. a *bitter* lesson = unforgettable

B. HIGH

1. a *high* hand = cruel 2. a *high* life = full of pleasure
3. the *Almighty* = God 4. *high* summer = in full swing
5. *high* words = angry 6. *high* time = proper time

C. TALL

1. a *tall* claim = unreasonable
2. a *tall* demand = too high
3. a *tall* story = unbelievable
4. a *tall* talk = boastful
5. a *tall* tongue = abusive
6. a *tall* walk = full of pride

D. WHITE

1. a *white* elephant = expensive mate
2. a *white* head = old age
3. a *white* lie = total lie
4. a *white* night = sleepless

E. SIMPLE

1. *simple* beauty = without make-up
2. *simple* heart = innocent
3. *simple* living = with few needs
4. *simple* mind = not cunning
5. *simple* truth = hard truth
6. *simple* problem = easy

V. ANTONYMS

Words	Antonyms	Words	Antonyms
able	unable	high	low
absent	present	import	export
active	inactive	like	dislike
add	subtract	large	small
agree	disagree	little	big
bold	timid	make	mar
brave	cowardly	noisy	quiet
broad	narrow	pure	impure
bright	dull	rural	urban
cold	hot	seldom	often
cool	warm	sell	buy
dry	wet	sink	float
easy	difficult	swim	drown
equal	unequal	sweet	bitter
fast	slow	top	bottom
fair	unfair	true	false
grateful	ungrateful	vice	virtue
heavy	light	wise	silly

VI. SMALLER PIECES

1.	a **chip** of wood	6.	a **crump** of bread
2.	a **scrap** of paper	7.	a **grain** of sand
3.	a **pinch** of salt	8.	a **morsel** of food
4.	a **wink** of sleep	9.	a **puff** of wind
5.	a **stump** of a cigarette	10.	a **sip** of water, milk

VII. ABBREVIATIONS

1.	**a.m.**	ante-meridian (fore-noon)
2.	**p.m.**	post meridian (after-noon)
3.	**AD**	Anno Domini (in the year of Our Lord)
4.	**BC**	Before Christ
5.	**Capt.**	Captain
6.	**Col.**	Colonel
7.	**DC**	Deputy Commissioner
8.	**Gen.**	General
9.	**Dr**	Doctor
10.	**Mr**	Mister
11.	**Ms**	Miss/Mistress (read Miz)
12.	**Mrs**	Mistress (read Misiz)
13.	**GPO**	General Post Office
14.	**MP**	Member of the Parliament
15.	**RMS**	Railway Mail Service

VIII. COMMON PHRASES

1.	**look for**	*seek*	I was *looking for* you there.
2.	**look down upon**	*hate*	Don't *look down upon* the poor.
3.	**put up with**	*bear*	I cannot *put up with* such insults.
4.	**go on**	*continue*	*Go on* with your work.
5.	**get down**	*alight*	I will *get down* at Tokyo.
6.	**go up**	*rise*	Prices are *going up* every day.
7.	**set out**	*proceed*	They *set out* on a long journey.
8.	**set in**	*begin*	Summer season has *set in*.

9.	**act upon**	*practise*	I shall *act upon* your advice.
10.	**live on**	*feed on*	Cows and horses *live on* grass.
11.	**put off**	*take off*	*Put off* this dirty dress.
12.	**stand by**	*help*	I shall always *stand by* you.
13.	**break down**	*be worse*	Her health is *breaking down* slowly.
14.	**break up**	*close*	The meeting will *break up* at 2-00 p.m.
15.	**call on**	*go to see*	He *called on* him yesterday.
16.	**call at**	*visit*	I *called at* his house yesterday.
17.	**die of**	*die due to*	The poor beggar *died of* hunger.
18.	**come of**	*belong to*	Nancy *comes of* a high family.
19.	**come about**	*happen*	How did it *come about* ?
20.	**call for**	*need*	The situation *calls for* patience.

IX. ONE WORD FOR MANY

1.	an animal with two feet	biped
2.	an animal with four feet	quadruped
3.	a disease/wound that ends in death	fatal
4.	a person lacking knowledge	ignorant
5.	one who can read and write	literate
6.	one who cannot read and write	illiterate
7.	that can be seen	visible
8.	that cannot be seen	invisible
9.	that can be divided	divisible
10.	that cannot be divided	indivisible
11.	that can be heard	audible
12.	that cannot be heard	inaudible
13.	that can be eaten	edible/eatable
14.	that cannot be eaten	inedible
15.	a child who has lost its parents	orphan
16.	a woman whose husband has died	widow
17.	a man whose wife has died	widower
18.	a person who is always in time	punctual
19.	that can be easily read	legible
20.	that cannot be easily read	illegible

X. SYNONYMS

Words		Synonyms	Words		Synonyms
1.	rich	wealthy	11.	pretty	beautiful
2.	thick	dense	12.	humble	polite
3.	hear	listen	13.	joy	happiness
4.	error	mistake	14.	sorrow	sadness
5.	gain	profit	15.	hate	dislike
6.	famous	known	16.	build	make
7.	quick	fast	17.	tell	describe
8.	old	ancient	18.	wind	air
9.	new	modern	19.	beauty	charm
10.	high	tall	20.	brave	valiant

XI. DISEASES

asthma	cholera	malaria	dysentery
influenza	typhoid	pneumonia	smallpox

XII. GAMES WHERE PLAYED

	Game	Where Played		Game	Where Played
1.	badminton	court	7.	race, golf	course
2.	chess	board	8.	hockey	field
3.	football	ground	9.	wrestling	arena
4.	boxing	ring	10.	tennis	court
5.	cricket	pitch	11.	skating	rink
6.	gymnastics	gymnasium	12.	carom	board

XIII. ELECTION TERMS

1.	polling booth	6.	a straight contest
2.	ballot box	7.	three-cornered contest
3.	ballot paper	8.	polling agent
4.	constituency	9.	polling officer
5.	by-election	10.	to forfeit one's deposit

XIV. NEWSPAPER TERMS

1. **news hawker**—person who sells newspapers
2. **editor**—person who edits a newspaper
3. **sub-editor**—person who does editing job as guided by an editor
4. **correspondent**—person who sends news to a newspaper
5. **editorial**—commentary piece written by an editor himself

XV. PROVERBS

1. A rolling stone gathers no moss.
2. As you sow, so shall you reap.
3. Empty vessels make much noise.
4. Everybody's business is nobody's business.
5. Example is better than precept.
6. A bird in the hand is worth two in the bush.
7. Prevention is better than cure.
8. Procrastination is the thief of time.
9. There is many a slip between the cup and the lip.
10. Nothing venture, nothing have.
11. No pains, no gains.
12. Honesty is the best policy.
13. Ill news runs apace.
14. Pride hath a fall.
15. Truth triumphs in the long run.
16. Where there is a will, there is a way.
17. Too many cooks spoil the broth.
18. Many a little makes a mickle.
19. A stitch in time saves nine.
20. A coward dies many times before his death.
21. Tomorrow is an old deceiver.
22. Hope sustains life.
23. Never put off till tomorrow what you can do today.
24. New brooms sweep clean.
25. Grief is a species of idleness.

A. PICTURE COMPOSITION

Picture composition *is a writing based on a given picture*. After observing the *persons, animals* and *objects* in the picture, an idea is formed about what the picture shows. A title is given to the picture and a composition is written on it.

THE FOX AND THE GRAPES

Look at the picture given. The picture shows a fox trying to pluck a bunch of grapes from the vineyard. The fox jumps to pluck the grapes from the branches, but he failed to get any grapes. He ran fast from quite a distance and made a flying leap at the grapes. He failed to get them. So, he ran faster in order to leap higher. But still, he could not get at the grapes. He was so tired after several attempts that he had to give up plucking the grapes. As he was not able to attain his goal, he remarked, that the grapes were indeed sour.

TEST YOURSELF

A. Observe this picture and write 10 sentences on it in your note-book :

1. OUR ENGLISH TEACHER

I study in St. Stephen School, New York. It is a very big school with 1500 students and a large number of teachers. It has a three storey building and a large playground.

I study in Grade IV. Jennifer teaches us English. She is our class teacher too. She is a tall, fair and slim lady. She is a highly qualified teacher with a very good command of English.

Our English teacher is very kind and polite. At the same time, she is very strict. She loves discipline. She teaches us with love and care. Her voice is impressive. She creates interest in our minds for her lessons. All other teachers hold her in high respect because of her ability.

Jennifer is in charge of the school dramatic club also. She stages one play every month. She prepares us for it very well through rehearsals. She helps us whenever we need her advice. She often tells us to learn good habits and manners. Jennifer is an ideal teacher. We all like her very much. She also loves us all.

TEST YOURSELF

A. Write an essay on each of the following :

    1. Our Sports Teacher   2. Our Principal   3. My Best Friend

2. A WALK IN THE MOONLIGHT

The moon has no light of its own. It shines with the light of the sun. Sunlight falls on the moon and it absorbs its heat. So, it reflects cold light in the sky. That is why moonlight is cool and pleasant. This light falls on the earth also.

A walk in moonlight is very soothing. Moonlight feels cool and pleasant. So, it refreshes the body as well as the mind. We feel relieved after walking in moonlight.

I am a regular walker in the morning as well as in the evening. I take a regular walk along a canal early in the morning. Again, I have a regular walk after having my dinner in the evening.

For more than half of every month, the nights are moonlit. So, I have a walk in moonlight I feel quite refreshed and relieved. The coolness of moonlight is very pleasing and soothing. It relieves all the tension of the day's work and makes the mind fresh. At the same time, it refreshes the body from head to foot.

TEST YOURSELF

1. A Morning Walk
2. A Visit to a Circus Show
3. A Visit to the Zoo
4. A Sleepless Night in Summer

1.   THE BEE AND THE DOVE

Once upon a time, a bee was flying about in search of honey. Suddenly, it felt thirsty. So, it flew to a nearby stream. But as soon as it tried to drink water, the current of water carried it away. Before long, it was going to be drowned.

Luckily for the bee, a peepal tree stood on the bank of the stream. A dove was sitting on one of its branches. The dove saw the drowning bee and decided to help it. At once she plucked a dry leaf of the peepal tree and flew to the bee. It placed the leaf just near the bee. The bee struggled hard and got onto the leaf. Soon its wings were dry and it flew off to safety. But the first thing that it did was to go to the dove and thank her.

A few days rolled by peacefully. One day, a hunter came into the forest for game. Till sunset, he could hunt no animal. Suddenly, he saw the dove and aimed an arrow at it. As the dove got ready to fly away, she saw a hawk hovering over the tree. So, she could not fly away.

Luckily for the dove, the bee happened to come there. Seeing the dove's life in danger, it lost no time and stung the hunter hard at his right hand. The hunter jerked his right arm and the arrow went off the bow missing its aim. It hit the hawk that fell down dead on the ground.

Finding herself quite safe, the dove flew away leaving the hunter helpless and sad. When she met the bee, she thanked her for saving her life.

Moral : *Do good, receive good.*

2. THE WOLF AND THE CRANE

Once upon a time, a wolf killed a hare. He enjoyed its tender flesh very much. But unluckily, a small bone got stuck into his throat. The wolf felt upset as he suffered acute pain in his throat because of the bone. Finding the pain intolerable, the wolf went about in search of a bird with a long beak. Before long, he came to a big pool and saw a big white crane standing on one leg in water.

He requested the crane to help him. He said, "Mr Crane ! I am in grave trouble. A bone has got stuck in my throat. Please take it out with your long beak. I am dying of pain".

"What will you give me for that ?" asked the crane.

"I will give you a good reward," replied the wolf.

"What after all ? Let me know," asked the crane again.

"I'll invite you to a delicious dinner," replied the wolf.

So, the crane put his long beak into the wolf's mouth and drew the bone out of his throat. The wolf felt relieved and thanked the crane.

"When are you inviting me to dinner Mr Wolf ?" asked the crane.

"Which dinner ?" retorted the wolf curtly.

"The one you promised just a short time ago," said the crane.

"Thank your stars, Mr Crane. Have you ever heard or seen a bird alive after putting its beak into a wolf's mouth ? You are quite safe. Isn't it a reward in itself ?"

The crane thought it wise to slink away from there. It left the place before anything untoward could happen.

Moral : *The wicked are never grateful.*

A. **Develop each of the following outlines into a readable story :**

1. A cunning fox........falls into a shallow well........cannot come out........ curses its lot........suddenly a goat comes........asks the fox why it is there........the fox replies, "To drink cold water." ....asks the goat to come down........the silly goat jumps down........the fox climbs onto the goat's back........comes out of the well........goat left there.

2. High summer........a lion lying asleep........a mouse jumps onto the lion's body........the lion disturbed........catches the mouse........decides to kill it........ the mouse requests to be spared........promises to repay the kindness........ set free........the lion caught in a net........tries to be free........cannot........ roars in anger........the mouse comes........ nibbles the net........frees the lion.

3. A shepherd living near a river........a narrow bridge over the river........ green pastures on both the banks........sheep and goats keep going from this bank to that........two goats come up the bridge from opposite sides........meet in the middle........cannot pass side by side........one goat lies down........the other passes over its body........the goats were wise.

B. **Look at each set of pictures and weave a readable story around it :**

1. Letter to a friend congratulating him on his brilliant result

J-128, Spring Street

New York

.... 2010

Dear Reggie,

I have received your letter dated 8th April today. I was extremely happy to know of your brilliant result in the annual examination. Accept my heartiest congratulations.

My parents also join me in congratulating you and they send their blessings also for your success in future. Convey our best wishes to all the members of your family.

Do keep in touch with me. I shall be looking forward to your next letter.

With best wishes once again.

Yours Sincerely,

John

2. Letter to uncle thanking him for his present on your birthday

St. Stephen School

117 Street, East Elmhurst

New York

.... 2010

Dear Uncle,

I have just received the wrist watch sent by you as my birthday present. Words really fail me to thank you for your deep love for me and for the precious present. Truly speaking, I was in dire need of a watch to be punctual. I am so proud of having a dear uncle like you. All my friends are praising you and your love for me.

Convey my respects to aunty and love to Mac and Nancy.

Thanking you once again.

Yours Affectionately,

Michael

3. Letter to father informing him about your test

Oxford School
68, Oak Street
New York
.... 2010

Dear father,

As promised to you, I am writing how I fared in my half yearly test. The test commenced on 20th of this month and went on up to 28th instant. I had prepared myself for the test fully. So, I have fared quite-well in all the papers. I really expect very high marks in every paper. As soon as I get my marks-sheet, I shall send its copy to you. I am quite hale and hearty by your blessings and God's grace. There is nothing to worry about.

Convey my respects to dear mother and dear grandma. Love to Katy and Peter. Ask them both to work hard at their studies.

Hoping to hear from you soon.

Yours Affectionately,

Steve

TEST YOURSELF

1. Write a letter to your father who is away on a business tour. Give him the home news.

2. Write a letter to your friend informing him of your standing first in the annual examination.

3. Write a letter to your younger brother asking him to work hard at his studies.

4. Write a letter to your mother asking her to take care of her health.

5. Write a letter to your sister informing her that you are sending her a fine dress by courier.

A paragraph on—HOW TO PREPARE A CUP OF TEA

Tea-making is not a difficult job at all. Take some water in a kettle and put it on fire. Put some tea leaves in the water and boil it for three minutes.

Boil milk in a separate kettle and put it in the milk pot. Put sugar in the sugar pot as well.

In order to prepare a cup of tea, fill about three-fourths of a cup with tea water. Then put milk and sugar into the cup according to your liking. Stir it with a spoon so that the sugar dissolves in it. The tea is ready for drinking.

TEST YOURSELF

A. Look at this picture and write a paragraph on —

HOW TO MEND A PENCIL

....

....

....

....

....

....

....

....

....

....

....

....

Comprehension means to read and understand an unseen passage and answer the questions given about its contents. Let us have an example :

One day a mouse inadverently woke up a lion from his sleep. The lion was extremely annoyed at the mouse's behaviour and decided to kill him. The mouse asked for pardon and promised to help the lion in times of distress. One day the lion was trapped in a hunter's net and could not free himself. The mouse came to his rescue by gnawing at the hunter's net and thereby set the lion free.

QUESTIONS :
1. What did the mouse do to the lion ?
2. Why was the lion angry ?
3. What did the lion decide to do ?
4. How did the mouse help the trapped lion ?

ANSWERS :
1. The mouse woke up the lion from his sleep.
2. The mouse had disturbed the lion's sleep.
3. The lion decided to kill the mouse.
4. The mouse gnawed at the hunter's net and set the lion free.

TEST YOURSELF

A. Read the paragraph and answer the questions given at its end :

The Niagra Falls is one of the largest falls in the world. It is situated in America bordering USA and Canada. Many tourists visit the Niagra for its sheer beauty. It is known for its scenic beauty, attractive thousands of tourists from all around the world. A transparent winch takes the tourist to the bottom of the falls to enable to get an even more majestic scenery.

QUESTIONS :
1. Which is the largest falls in the world ?
2. Where is the Niagra Falls located ?
3. Why is it famous ?
4. What is the arrangement available for the tourist to appreciate its majestic scenery ?